Montana Territory
Pioneer Recipes
&
Trivia

by
Louise Shafer

Montana Territory Pioneer Recipes & Trivia
by Louise Shafer

Copyright 1998
1st Edition 1998
Revised Edition 2016

Pioneer Publishing
4605 Argenta Rd.
Dillon, Montana 59725
or at bookpub16@gmail.com

ISBN: 978-0-9976114-0-3

Pioneer Publishing
4605 Argenta Rd.
Dillon, Montana 59725

Printed in the United States

Preface

The Montana Territory Pioneer Recipes & Trivia cookbook is an effort of the Jolly Jills Women's Club of Dillon, Montana. Over the years many local women have been involved in this club. The remaining and current members of the club are Carolyn Adams, Aileen Warrick, Betty Hanson and Louise Shafer. It is an organization of women that has met for many years in friendship and fellowship to support each other and their community.

The ladies learned the ways of their mothers, grandmothers, and great grandmothers as young girls. These ways had been passed from generation to generation and with this book they will give current and future generations a glimpse of times past. These ladies have cooked on the wood stoves, lived without electricity or phones and without indoor plumbing. They have experienced the way of life that is described in this book. Although they are thankful for the modern conveniences, they hold fond, and some not so fond, memories of times past. With this book they share some of the past with you and some stark differences of how it is today.

Over the years this group of ladies has given many educational programs to others to assist in countless helpful ways. They have done many fund raisers to support community members and projects. One of their primary fundraisers was done during the annual Bannack Days at Bannack, Montana, the first territorial capital of the Montana Territory, where they sold jams, jellies, cookies, cakes, pies and lemonade. In visiting with people during Bannack Days they discovered people wanted to know more about "the good old days" and how people did things and how they lived. That is how the Montana Territory Pioneer Recipes & Trivia cookbook came into being.

The funds from the sale of the Montana Territory Pioneer Recipes & Trivia cookbook have been and are the primary source of monies to support many community endeavors. They have donated money to many community causes but their primary project has been the New Born Book Project. Children's books are presented to new parents with the goal of encouraging the parents to read to their children and thus introduce children to the joys of reading and learning.

Introduction

Gold was first discovered in Bannack on July 28, 1862 by John White. He filed on this claim on August 30, 1862, the first claim to be taken. People not only came to mine but also to ranch. Records show that parcels were being taken up near Bannack on the Grasshopper, on the Beaverhead, on the Horse Prairie and other areas for ranching purposes.

Living conditions were very primitive at best. If the miners and their families came in a covered wagon they may have had a small stove to cook on, otherwise cooking was done on a camp fire. There were no houses in the beginning, just tents, wagons, willow huts, a hole in a bank or whatever other shelter they could quickly put up. There were trees nearby and by winter some cabins were constructed but the winter of 1862-63 was very hard for the people who came to get rich. The first death recorded in Bannack was on October 2, 1862 of W. H. Bell who reportedly died of typhoid fever. Along with death came the birth of the first white child in December of 1862 to the wife of S.B. Burchett.

By spring provisions were being freighted in from Fort Benton, 300 miles north or Salt Lake City, Utah, 300 miles south of Bannack. By the end of the summer of 1863 many houses and businesses were built and life was much easier. Now, you could buy some staples right in Bannack to cook with. Flour was $40.00 for a 100 pound sack, and sugar, coffee and bacon were $1.00 a pound. On November 21, 1863 they even got a post office in Bannack.

In May of 1863 another gold discovery was made in Alder Gulch by the Fairweather/Edger party. By June 1863 Virginia City was founded and the rush was on to the new discoveries. Both areas and towns continued to grow and prosper. At this time this was Idaho Territory by an act of Congress in March of 1863. It would become Montana Territory in May of 1864. In July 1864 gold was discovered in Last Chance Gulch, the future site of Helena. Over the years other discoveries were made and towns like Montana, now Argenta, where the first smelter in the territory was built, were settled. Marysville, Emigrant, Elkhor Garnet, Hecla, Rochester, Dewey, Highland City, Red Lodge, Ny Butte, Anaconda are just a few names of other discoveries ar settlements in the territory and what would, in 1889, become the State Montana. People were on the move, looking for bigger and better things Think back to the beginning of all of this. Imagine coming by hor and wagon, on horseback or walking from faraway places such as Sa Lake City, Utah, Fort Benton, Montana or elsewhere and having prepare meals with only what you could bring with you, collect or hun Most of the staple foods carried were flour, meal, salt, sugar or molass and some dried beans, corn and fruits. All else had to be gotten from th land. Meat was rabbits, deer, fish, ducks, sage chicken, buffalo, antelop elk or whatever was available that had to be hunted. No refrigeration wa available or no store to go to. Large animals were hunted, butchered an shared. This was summer in the Territory so there were wild plants tha could be gathered but remember, these people came here to mine fc gold which probably did not leave a lot of time to gather all these thing that were available to eat. The men with families were far better off a the family could do the gathering while the men worked the claim.

The men and women that settled the frontier struggled and worke for a better life. Women took care of their families and homes. With thi book it is hoped to show what it took, on the women's part, day to day to survive and prosper. Women's work was never done and require many skills and much labor. − *Louise Shafer*

Table of Contents

Here's To the Women

Here's to the women who led the way,
That made us what we are today.
They braved the wilds of the wilderness,
seeking a life of happiness.
Raising their families as they went,
as though it was all heaven meant.

These women one and all,
regardless of their regal call,
carried their load and dared to roam,
to better their cause and have a new home.

We give three cheers for the women of old
who made the story we've just told,
who furthered our cause and journeyed far,
to seek better things than they had so far.

Can we pick up the load and do our part,
to continue the work they gave a start?

Here's to the women of today,
who will carry the load and show the way
to further the cause and carry it on,
so others may delight in what went on.

Women of tomorrow will rally, of course,
and continue the work from their very own source
and carry it out to the very end,
fixing all fences that they can mend.

- Louise Shafer

BEVERAGES

Coffee

There was Cowboy Coffee, Sodbuster Coffee, Chuck Wagon Coffee, Sheepherder Coffee, or maybe the housewife's specialty. All of the settlers had a variety of ways of making coffee. They bought the hole beans, unroasted, and had to roast them on a stove or over the ampfire and then grind the coffee as they needed it.

Some of the variations might have been to put a little salt in the coffee s it will bring out the flavor. If you are cooking coffee on a camp fire, lay stick over the top of your coffee pot and the coffee will not boil over. It said to put an egg shell in your coffee if you have hard water and for avor.

A coffee recipe from the *1913 Tested Recipes, by the Ladies Aid ociety, 1st Baptist Church, Dillon*, **Montana** states:

Allow 1 tablespoon of coffee to each cup, also 1 for the pot; mix with gg and little cold water, let come to a boil, add as many cups boiling rater less 1 as there are tablespoonful of coffee; let boil 5 minutes, set ack on stove and steep for a few minutes or until it pours clear from the pout.

As you can see from the following article there are rays of stretching coffee!

Hard Times Coffee

Jerry Huggins, a retired truck driver, has revived what he calls "hard imes coffee," a blend of coffee beans and barley grains popular in certain reas during the Great Depression four decades ago.

"It's good and it's cheap," Huggins said. "What more can you ask or?"

He occasionally makes a pot of "coffee" just from barley, but more often mixes equal portions of the grains with his usual off-the-shelf coffee o come up with a dark steamy drink that tastes just like coffee but costs arely half as much.

He roasts the barley in the oven at 400° for 45 minutes, stirring the grains so they don't scorch. When the grains are deep brown, he puts them n an antique coffee grinder, but a blender works just as well. Then mix it

1

with regular coffee to taste and brew it as usual.

Huggins said he pays about six cents a pound for barley.

"You can get it anywhere out in the country," he says, "Find a fe elevator or a friendly farmer. Just make sure it's malting barley."

-Excerpts taken from an article in the Montana Standard, Bu Montana- date unknown

Home Brew Beer

6 gallons water   1 cup brown sugar
1 can malt syrup   1 cake yeast

Let stand in warm room for 60 hours, and then skim. Bottle - place teaspoon white sugar in each bottle. Cap Jars.

Cottage Beer

Put a peck of good wheat bran and 3 handfuls of hops into 10 gallo of water and boil together until the bran and hops sink to the bottom. Then strain it through a thin cloth into a cooler and add 2 quarts of molasses when it is about lukewarm. As soon as the molasses is dissolved, pour the mixture into a ten-gallon cask and add 2 tablespoonfuls of yeast. When fermentation is over with, cork up the cask and it will be ready for use in four or five days.

Dandelion Wine
(4 quarts)

3 quarts chopped dandelion flowers   1 gallon water
6 cups sugar   1 cake yeast

Use a crock. Bring water to boil, add 1/2 sugar or 3 cups. Pla dandelions in crock, pour hot water over them, allow to cool. When co add yeast, cover crock, let stand 5 to 6 days. Add remaining sugar, cove let stand until fermentation ceases, a little over a week. Strain and bottle.

Chokecherry Wine

Pick chokecherries when fully ripe. Crush or grind. Use about 2 1/2 gallons of berries - measured after crushed. Add 1 gallon water. Let stand 24 hours, strain. Add sugar. The amount of sugar used depends on how sweet you want the wine. For a very sweet wine use about 9 cups of sugar. If you want a dryer wine use less sugar but you have to have sugar for fermentation to take place. Cover and keep in warm room. Let ferment about two weeks or until fermentation ceases. Strain and bottle.

Rhubarb Wine

Rhubarb makes a very excellent wine, which when it has stood for a sufficient length of time acquires a flavor like that of champagne. If it is made as soon as rhubarb is plentiful it may be used the following Christmas, though it improves with age. To 10 pounds cut rhubarb add 2 gallons water. The rhubarb should be bruised with a heavy weight so the juice will come out readily. After, adding the water let it stand five days, stirring occasionally. Add 8 pounds of sugar and the rind of 2 lemons to the strained juice. Let this ferment 4 or 5 days more, adding to it on the second day 1/2 ounce of gelatin to aid in clearing. At the end of 5 days skim any crust which may have formed from the top, and put the wine in a cask. Do not cork the 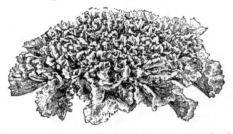 cask but leave the bung open until 2 weeks have gone by. Then cork the cask and let the wine remain for six months before bottling. The bottles should stand for a month at least before the wine is used. - A Friend - *1913 Tested Recipes, by the Ladies Aid Society, 1st Baptist Church, Dillon, Montana*

Raisin Wine

Two pounds of raisins seeded and chopped fine, 1 pound of sugar, 1 lemon and about 2 gallons of boiling water. Put into a stone jar and stir daily for 6 to 8 days; then strain and bottle and put in a cool place for 10 days and it will be ready to use. - *The People's Home Recipe Book by Mrs. Alice G. Kirk, 1913*

Hard Cider

Add sugar and yeast to apple juice and allow to ferment. Strain ar bottle.

Apple Juice

Take fresh, ripe apples, wash, quarter and core. Put in an apple pre and squeeze or crush. You will get juice and some pulp. If pulp is n desired, the juice may be strained through a cloth. Drink as it is squeeze or cool and drink.

Gooseberry Juice Drink

Pick ripe gooseberries. Wash and crush. Strain juice through a cloth dilute with water as if making lemonade. Add sugar to taste. Chill an serve. - *Bertha (Knapp) Shafer from Louise Shafer Collection*

Snow Cup

If you can find a snow drift, dig down and get some clean snow in cup, pour sweetened gooseberry juice over the snow and 'presto' yo have a "Snow Cup".

Blackberry Cordial

One quart juice, 1 pound sugar, 1 tablespoon each of cinnamor allspice and cloves. Boil 15 minutes. To keep some time, put in tablespoons brandy. - A Friend - *1913 Tested Recipes, by the Ladies Ai Society, 1st Baptist Church, Dillon, Montana*

Tip . . .

Fruit stains may be removed from table linen by pouring boiling water through the cloth where it i stained.

4

BREADS

When the large herds of cattle were being driven from place to place or the pioneers were crossing the plains and settling in unsettled remote areas, it was impossible to have a ready supply of many things. One was the availability of yeast. They did not have the nice neat packages of yeast we have today, therefore they relied on sourdough and the  ongoing leavening it made available to them. Most of the homes had a crock with sourdough in it. They took great care to keep it active and used it every day for many of their meals.

Yeast

Where did yeast bread originate? No one really knows for sure. Perhaps today's light bread owes its beginnings to someone who mixed a forgotten dough with a fresh batch and ended up with a light, delicious bread due to the development of yeast in the older dough. Was this in China, Egypt, Rome or perhaps some other far away time and place? This was an unrecorded event but indeed led to the wonderful flavors and goodness of today's bread. Yeast is the key to our breads as we know them today.

Yeast is the leavening for breads. It makes the dough rise and the bread light. Yeast is a living plant that thrives on the sugar in the dough, producing gas that makes the yeast dough and batters rise. It also gives them a delicious flavor and aroma.

Sourdough Starter

2 cups flour in a crock, or jar   2 1/2 cups lukewarm water

Mix well and set, covered, in a warm place. In about four or five days the mixture will be bubbly. This mixture has produced its own yeast and is now ready for you to use.

You can use this starter in sourdough recipes as the old timers did or you can "hurry it up" and add yeast as in the Modern Basic Sourdough Starter recipe. If you do not add the yeast it takes longer to make your bread, etc., but it is well worth the wait and you do not have the expense of buying yeast.

5

Tip . . .

Do not use chlorinated water in your sourdough as it will affect he the yeast works.

Basic Sourdough Bread
(Without adding yeast)

Night before take:

2 cups starter in warm bowl
2 cups warm water and/or milk
2 cups flour

The next morning add:

2 tablespoons shortening
2 teaspoons salt
1 teaspoon soda
flour as needed

Mix all of the above and add enough flour to make a sponge. Let rai in warm place to near double in bulk. Add flour enough to make a dou, that can be kneaded. Knead and place back in bowl and let raise to doub Make loaves, let raise, and bake at 350° for 30 to 40 minutes.

Eggs may be added if you want a different type of bread. Also t adding oatmeal, other grains, nuts, or dried fruit.

How long to prepare bread this way will depend on how active yo starter is and if you keep everything warm for the raising process.

Tip . . .

If your starter molds it is ruined - toss it and start over!!
If starter turns orange, throw it away!

Sourdough Pancakes

2 cups starter
2 eggs
2 tablespoons oil
1/4 to 1/2 cup milk (enough to make batter thin)
1 teaspoon salt
1 teaspoon baking soda
1 tablespoon sugar

Let rest 10 to 15 minutes before frying.

Sourdough Waffles

Use same as for pancakes; only add 2 extra tablespoons oil and more sugar and eggs, if desired.

Tip . . .

Please feed your starter. **Don't forget to add warm water and flour back to your starter to replenish your supply.**

Tip . . .

Do not put back anything in your starter but flour or water. If you add sugar, salt, eggs, soda or cooking oil it will ruin the starter.

Unrivaled Yeast

One morning boil two ounces of the best hops in four quarts of water half an hour; strain it, and let the liquor cool to the consistency of new milk; then put it in an earthen bowl and add half a cupful of salt and half a cupful of brown sugar; beat up one quart of flour with some of the liquor; then mix all well together, and let it stand till the third day after; then add six medium-sized potatoes, boiled and mashed through a colander; let it stand a day, then strain and bottle and it is fit for use. It must be stirred frequently while it is making, and kept near a fire. One advantage of this yeast is its spontaneous fermentation, requiring the help of no old yeast; if care is taken to let it ferment well in the bowl, it may immediately be corked tightly. Be careful to keep it in a cool place. Before using it shake the bottle up well. It will keep in a cool place two months, and is best the latter part of the time. Use about the same quantity as of other yeast. - *The White House Cook Book, copyright 1887.*

Dried Yeast or Yeast Cakes

Make a pan of yeast; mix in with it corn meal that has been sifted and dried, kneading it well until it is thick enough to roll out, then it can be cut into cakes or crumble up. Spread out and dry thoroughly in the shade; keep in a dry place. - *The White House Cook Book, copyright 1887.*

Salt-Raising Bread

While getting breakfast in the morning, as soon as the tea-kettle boiled, take a quart tin cup or an earthen quart milk pitcher, scald it, th fill one-third full of water about as warm as the finger could be held then to this add a teaspoonful of salt, a pinch of brown sugar and co flour enough to make a batter of about the right consistency for gridd cakes. Set the cup, with the spoon in it, in a closed vessel half-filled w water moderately hot, but not scalding. Keep the temperature as nea even as possible, and add a teaspoonful of flour once or twice during t process of fermentation. The yeast ought to reach to the top of the bowl about five hours.

Sift your flour into a pan, make an opening in the centre, and pour your yeast. Have ready a pitcher of warm milk, salted, or milk and wat (not too hot or you will scald the yeast germs,) and stir rapidly into pulpy mass with a spoon. Cover this sponge closely, and keep warm an hour, then knead into loaves, adding flour to make the prop consistency. Place in warm, well-greased pans, cover closely, and lea till it is light. Bake in a steady oven, and when done let all the hot stea escape. Wrap closely in damp towels, and keep in closed earthen jars un it is wanted.

This, in our grandmother's time, used to be considered the pri bread, on account of its being sweet and wholesome, and required prepared yeast to make it. - *Betty Hanson*

THEN: To make bread in the early days you had to prepare in advan because you had to make or "develop" your own yeast. This could done by several methods. Some methods called for potatoes, others hop still others milk and others may be a combination of ingredients. All ha to have salt.

NOW: Nowadays yeast bread is made with very little trouble, as Fleischmann's yeast can be procured at almost any grocery or go to the bakery department of your favorite grocery and buy the bread you want. - *Betty Hanson*

Modern Basic Sourdough Starter

Starter: 3 cups white flour
        1 package dry yeast
        2 1/2 cups lukewarm water

Night before, mix with starter
        2 cups lukewarm water
        2 1/2 cups flour

Next morning, take out 1 cup and keep as starter. Store starter in glass jar, covered in refrigerator. The old timers, not having refrigeration, kept the crock in a cool area of the home or in a cool pantry area.

Modern Sourdough Bread

1 cup starter	1 tablespoon dry yeast
2 cups water	4 cups whole wheat flour
4 cups unbleached flour	1/4 cup wheat germ
2 cups milk	1 teaspoon salt
2 teaspoons honey	1 teaspoon baking soda

Combine starter, 2 cups warm water, 2 cups unbleached flour in a large bowl, cover and let stand 8 to 12 hours. This is called a sponge. It will be bubbly when ready to use. Scald milk, stir in honey and allow to cool to lukewarm. Sprinkle yeast into milk and stir until dissolved. Combine this with the sponge. Add 2 cups whole wheat flour and wheat germ, mix well, sprinkle salt and baking soda into the dough and stir gently. Cover and let raise about 30 minutes. Add flour until dough is very stiff. Knead 8 minutes on a floured surface. Divide in half and shape into loaves. Place in loaf pan, let raise until double. Bake at 400° for 20 minutes. Reduce heat to 325°, bake until done. Bread will pull away from the sides of the pan and sound hollow when thumped on top.

Oatmeal Bread

To 3 cups of oat meal add 3 cups boiling water, 1/2 cup molasses, salt and 1 yeast cake, set at noon. At night knead hard by adding white flour. Let rise until morning. Put into pans and bake when light.

9

Buns

Set in the evening, 1 pint of milk, butter the size of an egg, tablespoons of yeast, and flour enough to make a thick batter. In th morning add 2 eggs, 4 tablespoons of sugar and flour enough to roll ou after mixing, let stand till quite light. Then make into buns and let rise hours and bake 15 minutes.

Apple Fritters

Make the "Buns" above or use a regular bread recipe. Peel two or thre medium apples, dice and knead them into th dough. Let dough raise and then pinch o small amounts of dough, punch down an flatten.

Place grease in a pan to about 3 inches dee Heat grease and when hot place the flattene dough in the grease. Cook until brown, tur and brown on other side. Remove from greas drain and then toss in sugar and cinnamor Serve warm.

Tip . . .

If you want a glaze instead of sugar and cinnamon on your appl fritter, mix 1 teaspoon butter, 1 cup powdered sugar and enough mil for a consistency of cream. Frost while fritter is hot.

French Toast

2 eggs
1/2 teaspoon salt

2/3 cup milk
6 slices of stale bread

Beat eggs slightly, add salt and milk. Dip the bread in mixture. Hav griddle hot and well buttered; brown the bread on each side. Serve ho with sugar or syrup.

Cream or Milk Toast

2 cups milk or cream   2 tablespoons butter
1 tablespoon flour   1 teaspoon salt

Cook the flour in melted butter. Add salt and gradually stir in hot milk. After it thickens, pour this sauce over slices of dry or water toast. Serve hot.

Quicker way:

Butter the dry hot toast, add 1/2 tablespoon salt to one cup of hot milk, and pour it over the toast. Serve hot.

Tip . . .

To make water toast, dip a piece of toast quickly into boiling salted water, remove to dish, butter and serve.

Bread Griddle Cakes

Pour over one pint of stale bread crumbs one pint hot milk and add 1 tablespoon butter. When the crumbs are soft rub through a strainer. Add the beaten yolks of 2 eggs, 1 cup flour, 1/2 teaspoon salt and 2 teaspoons of baking powder. If batter is not thin enough, add a little cold milk. Cook on a hot skillet as you would a pancake.

For Housekeeping

"Take one part of self-control, one part discipline, 5 parts patience and sweeten all with charity". Keep constantly on hand and the domestic wheels will run smoothly. – *From the Ethyl Sorensen Collection*

The "How" To On Gardening

Most all soil will grow something. The creeks and river meadows w grow most things if the weather will cooperate. In Bannack a surrounding areas, the soil was good but the growing season short. Ma cool weather plants were grown there; cabbage, spinach cauliflower, pe carrots, onions, potatoes, lettuce, and radishes. Beans also would grow one was lucky enough to not get a late spring frost or an early fall frost. the early days the pioneers could not run to the "garden store" for th seeds. They brought the seeds with them on their trek west and then eve year they had to harvest enough seed from their gardens to be able replant the next year.

Most all homes raised what they could but it took some doing to g the garden prepared for planting. The garden plot had to be accessible water as there were no sprinklers and wells were few and far between. water could not be run to a garden in ditches it had to be carried in bucket to water the plants.

The garden plot had to be dug by hand with a shovel; sod turned over and left, preferably over winter, so the grass would die. If manure was available it was spread on the dug ground. It was then dug again and raked to make into a fine soil. Now it was ready to plant. The seeds would germinate in a short time if the soil was warm and damp, but also the weeds would come up and those had to be hoed down so the good plants had room to grow and mature. Radishes and lettuce were usually the fir vegetables ready to use, then peas. The others took longer to mature b by fall the whole garden was ready to harvest.

Now it had to be stored. Usually this was done in a root cellar th would not freeze during the cold winter. Most houses built in Bannac days had a hole dug under the floor with a trap door where things could b stored so they would not freeze or hole dug in a bank with a door on it.

It amazes me how they did so much with so little. - *Louise Shafer*

QUICK BREAD

Corn Bread

2 cups corn meal
2 tablespoons flour
2 tablespoons lard
2 heaping teaspoons
baking powder

2 cups sweet milk
2 heaping tablespoons sugar
2 eggs
1 large teaspoon salt

Mix all ingredients, pour into a heated pan and bake in hot oven 25 minutes.

Baking Powder Biscuits

3 cups flour
4 teaspoons baking powder
1 cup milk

1 teaspoon salt
6 tablespoons shortening

Mix flour, baking powder and salt. Cut in shortening. Add milk. Turn into lightly floured board, pat to 1/2 inch thick. Cut with cutter or water lass. Bake at 450° for 12 minutes or until golden brown.

Grandma's Biscuit Recipe

Two hands full of flour
Dab of lard
Tad of baking powder
Pinch of salt
Half pitcher of sweet milk

Mix well together flour, baking powder and salt. Add lard, cut in. Add milk, mix, pat or roll out to 1/2 inch thickness, cut and put in pan. Bake until rich golden brown.

How many biscuits you get depends upon the size of your "hands" full of flour and what size your pitcher is. If the pitcher is big you had better put a couple more "hands" full of flour in and a little extra of the other ingredients as well. Good luck and "pinch" careful!!

Master Biscuit Mix

For 13 cups

9 cups flour	1/3 cup baking powder
1 teaspoon salt	2 teaspoons cream of tartar
1/4 cup sugar	2 cups shortening

Sift dry ingredients 3 times. Cut in shortening and mix thorough Store in covered jars. If using lard use 1 3/4 cups. Use mix for biscui cookies, muffins, pancakes, waffles, etc. by adding milk and eggs create your desired product.

THEN: If you were an organized cook you would make your own bisc mix and put it away for later use. This was very handy to have but y had to take great care to keep it very cool and dry. If it warmed a amount or was kept for a long time you took the chance of yo shortening going rancid and thus ruining your prepared mix.

NOW: Go to your nearest store and purchase a bright yellow box Bisquick. - *Carolyn Adams*

Blueberry Buckle

3/4 cup sugar	1/4 cup soft shortening
1 egg	1/2 cup milk
2 cups flour	1/2 teaspoon salt
2 teaspoons baking powder	2 cups blueberries*

Heat oven to 375°. Mix sugar, shortening, egg. Stir in milk. S together and stir in dry ingredients. Blend in berries. Spread in greas and floured 9 inch square pan. Sprinkle with Crumb Topping. Bake 45 50 minutes or until toothpick thrust into center comes out clean. *Oth types of berries may be used.

Crumb Topping: Mix 1/2 cup sugar, 1/3 cup flour, 1/2 teaspo cinnamon and 1/4 cup soft butter.

Muffins

2 cups flour	1 cup milk
3 teaspoons baking powder	4 tablespoons sugar
3 tablespoons shortening	1/2 teaspoon salt
1 egg, well beaten	

Combine egg, shortening, milk and sugar. Add
dry ingredients. Beat until smooth. Grease muffin
tins, fill 2/3 full. Bake at 425° for 15 to 20 minutes.

Popovers

2 eggs, well beaten	1 cup flour
1/2 cup milk	salt
1/2 cup water	

Combine eggs, salt, and flour. Add water slowly and beat. Add milk,
continue beating until batter is smooth. Pour batter into hot, well oiled
pans. Bake at 425° for 40 to 60 minutes or until light and dry.

German Skillet Pancake

3 eggs, room temperature	1/2 cup flour
1/2 cup milk, room temperature	pinch of salt
cinnamon to taste, optional	
7 teaspoons (approximate) butter, oil or bacon grease	

Place a 10 inch cast iron skillet in the oven at 450° and heat until
skillet is very hot. Beat eggs until light, add remaining ingredients and
blend well. Add butter or oil to your hot skillet and let heat up. Pour
batter into skillet and return to oven immediately. Bake about 20 to 25
minutes until puffed up and golden brown. Serve immediately. The
pancake will flatten as it cools. Serve with butter and syrup. It also can be
served with just a sprinkling of powdered sugar.

Dutch Hotcakes

2 large eggs
1 1/4 cup milk
1 cup flour

pinch of salt
butter, oil or bacon grease

Blend all ingredients. Place oil or butter in a frying pan, and melt. Po
about three tablespoons of batter in hot oil. Spread out to a very thin laye
Fry until edges start to crisp and hotcake is golden, turn over and contin
to cook to a golden color. Serve with syrup, sugar or with fruit an
whipped cream. If batter is too thick add more milk until the consistenc
is right.

Improve Fat for Frying Doughnuts, Croquettes, Etc.

Fry out carefully 2 1/2 lbs. of beef suet, add 1 lb. of fresh lard. Aft
using, strain and put in small bucket and cover; may be used a number c
times. - *The Peoples Home Recipe Book by Mrs. Alice G. Kirk, 1913*

Doughnuts

"One cup of sugar, one cup of milk,
Two eggs beaten fine as silk,
Salt and nutmeg (lemon will do),
Of baking powder teaspoons two,
Lightly stir the flour in,
Roll on pie board not too thin;
Cut in diamonds, twist or rings,
Drop with care the doughy things
Into fat that briskly swells
Evenly the spongy cells;
Watch with care the time for turning,
Fry them brown just short of burning;
Roll in sugar, serve when cool,
Price a quarter for this rule."

By Hazel A Marquis

- *The Peoples Home Recipe Book by Mrs. Alice G. Kirk, 1913*

Cook'n on a Wood Stove

Cooking was done on a wood stove called a range. Many people today have a real fondness for these stoves but never have cooked on one. First thing in the morning the fire was built in the range, after the ashes from yesterday's fire were removed. Wood and kindling were usually in a wood box by the stove. Paper, if available, was crumpled up and kindling and wood laid on top, then set on 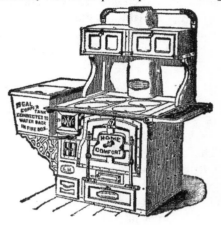 fire. As it burned down more wood was added until the range top and oven heated to the desired temperature. Everything needing heat was done on the range. The fire was kept burning most of the time. In winter the kitchen was always warm and cozy but summer it was unbearably hot so all cooking was planned and done as early as possible so the fire could burn out until needed in the evening. It is much easier today with gas and electric stoves just to turn the switch on or off, no wood or kindling to get, no ashes to empty, etc.

If the soot built up in the range chimney or stove pipe, it would smoke and darken your walls so about once a month the soot had to be removed and that was a real messy job and with no vacuum to clean it up with, it was a major cleaning chore. - *Les Riley*

Wood was the primary fuel source for the cook stove but when trees were scarce, grass or straw which was twisted tightly, were used as were "cow patties" (dried manure) and, if available, corn cobs.

How Did They Start The Fire?

Matches, as we know them today, were not readily available to the pioneers. Matches were indeed invented by the Chinese centuries back and "reinvented" in the early 1800's but were not stable and might light whenever or wherever and were considered dangerous. The "safety match" was fairly well perfected in the mid 1850's and by the 1860's there was limited availability to the general public. Safety matches would

only light when struck on a rough surface. Yes, matches were availa
but what if you did not have a match?

For many years prior to the match, obviously people were lighti
fires. They could use friction by rubbing sticks together to produce fire
they might have used a flint and steel. When flint and steel are stru
together a spark is created, lighting a fire using very fine, dry tinder. A
live embers were carried from campfire to campfire. They were kept
horn or shell containers, wrapped tightly to prevent bursting into flame.

A piece of thick glass also might be used to intensify the sun light a
start a fire but you had to have a sunny day, and of course, at night y
were left out in the cold. – *Myrna (Shafer) Carpita*

Store Bought Foods

When the pioneers came to the west in wagon trains, on foot
horseback they generally carried "staples" or basic food iten
These were foods that were easy to store and easy to prepare a
nutritious, but even better when various meats and wild edible plar
could be gathered along the trail and added for nutrition and flavor.

If they arrived very early to a new mining area, for instance, they h
to rely on what supplies they had with them and what they could glea
from the land as there still were not any stores. As time went on and mo
people arrived there were also enterprising individuals that brought
supplies and set up stores. This made it easier to get your food, if t
prices were not too high.

As stores and supply routes became more established then mo
variety of foods could be gotten. Many foods, such as prunes, date
raisins and different kinds of nuts could be had and added variety to one
diet. Of course flour, molasses and sugar could be purchased as cou
corn meal and various other whole grains.

As the country settled and the railroa
arrived on the frontier, the availability of foc
was far more plentiful and the area becan
more like we know it today, although tl
"store on the corner" was probably quite
ways away for the rancher and solitary miner

CANDY

Vinegar Taffy

2 cups sugar
2 tablespoons butter
few grains of salt

1/2 teaspoon cream of tarter
1/2 cup vinegar

Combine all ingredients. Boil to hard ball age. Let taffy cool just a bit, rub butter on your ınds and pull taffy until it sets up. Form into ▸ng strands and cut about one inch lengths. 'rap in waxed paper, twisting on both ends. affy pulls are a fun function for children and Juls alike. - *Louise Shafer*

Molasses Taffy

2 cups sugar
1 teaspoon soda

1 cup molasses
1 tablespoon vinegar

Boil until brittle and pull.

Tip . . .

Vhen pulling taffy coat your hands with butter. Candy will not stick ɔ your hands and burn you.

Patience Candy

3 cups granulated sugar
1 tablespoon butter

2 cups milk
1 cup pecans

Melt 1 cup of sugar in iron saucepan, stirring constantly until the onsistency of molasses. Add 1 cup milk and boil until the caramel is issolved; then add the rest of the milk, 2 cups of sugar and butter. Boil ntil it threads heavily when dropped from a spoon. Take from fire, stir ntil it hardens, add the nuts. Pour into buttered platter and when cool cut n squares.

19

Sea Foam

2 cups of granulated sugar   1/2 cup of corn syrup
1/2 cup of water   1 teaspoon of vanilla
1 cup of nuts   1 egg white

Boil sugar, syrup and water until it will form a soft ball when dropp
in cold water. Let stand a few minutes, add the beaten white of e
vanilla and nut meats. Beat 15 to 20 minutes. Pour or drop with spoon
buttered platter.

Fudge

Two squares of chocolate (cocoa will do), 3 cups of white sugar, an
1/2 cups of sweet cream. Boil until it forms a waxy ball when dropped
water. Let cool and beat until it thickens - pour into an oiled pan.

Panoche

One and a half cups of brown sugar, 1/2 cup of white sugar,
tablespoon of butter, and 2 teaspoons of milk. Place these ingredients i
granite pan, set over a good fire, and stir constantly for about fo
minutes. After it begins to boil test by dropping a bit in cold water, if
gets tough, but not brittle, it is done. Stir in 1 cup of shelled peanuts
walnuts and pour on buttered plates.

Marshmallows

Soak 1/2 box of gelatin in two thirds cup of tepid water. Take tv
cups of white sugar and two thirds cup of cold water. Boil sugar until
threads. When cool mix with gelatin and beat for fifteen minutes. - Lizz
Foote - *1913 Tested Recipes, by the Ladies Aid Society, 1st Bapt
Church, Dillon, Montana*

**Marshmallows were made at home in the old days. Then th
became a specialty item for the candy stores. The candy stores so
marshmallows packed in round and square tins. Some of the old ti
can be found in various collections and antique stores.**

Divinity

2 cups sugar
1/2 cup light corn syrup
1/2 cup water

Combine above in sauce pan. Cook, stirring until sugar dissolves, then cook over low heat, without stirring, to hard ball stage. Meanwhile put into large bowl:

2 egg whites
1/8 teaspoon salt

Beat until stiff but still moist, about 2 minutes. Slowly pour hot syrup over egg whites while continuing to beat until mixture thickens. Add 1 teaspoon vanilla and 1 cup nut meats (chopped). Beat until candy holds shape. Drop from teaspoons onto waxed paper - *Louise Shafer*

Food Coloring

If desired, the colors for candies may be made at home instead of being purchased at a confectionery.

For Red – Take one-half pint of water, add one ounce of cochineal and boil for five minutes and add one half once of powdered alum, one ounce of cream of tartar and boil for ten minutes. Take from stove and stir at once in two ounces of sugar and bottle for use.

For Blue – Rub indigo in a little water in a saucer.

For Yellow – Rub gamboge in water in same way.

For Green – Boil spinach leaves in a little water for one minute, strain and bottle. - *The Peoples Home Recipe Book by Mrs. Alice G. Kirk, 1913*

Rugs in the Pioneer Home

Many of the pioneer homes had rugs, yes, even on a dirt floor wi wooden stakes driven through the rug and into the dirt floor to ho the rug in place. In some cases they spread straw or rushes under the rug for softer walking and sleeping should someone have to sleep on the floor.

Some pioneer women brought the rugs with them or the rugs were made as time and materials allowed. The rugs were generally made from scraps of cloth that could not be used for anything else. The pieces of cloth were sewn together and

Wire Rug Beater

could either be woven on a loom or they could be braided together an then sewn in a round or oval shape. They added warmth and hominess t the pioneer home.

Having rugs was a nice addition to any home but how do you clea them? After all, there were no vacuums available. Well, as with all thing in pioneer times it was done with manual labor.

Weaving on a Loom

The rugs were taken out of the house an hung on a clothes line or fence and then carpet beater was used to beat the dirt an dust out of the rug, thus cleaning it. Onc cleaned the rugs were put back in the hom until the next cleaning session. The ru "beating" fell to the children of th household if they were big enough to do th job; otherwise the woman of the hous generally did this chore.

Carpet Bugs

To kill carpet bugs put one tablespoonful of corrosive sublimate into quart of hot water and saturate the floors and cracks in the walls. If th carpet is to be sponged, use a weaker solution. It will be found a sur treatment. - *The Peoples Home Recipe Book by Mrs. Alice G. Kirk 1913*

DAIRY PRODUCTS

Many of the settlers kept a milk cow. This gave them an ever ready supply of milk and fresh cream. The fresh milk and cream allowed them to make puddings, ice cream, cheese, cottage cheese, etc. The cream and milk were separated by letting the whole milk set and allowing the cream to rise to the top. The cream was then skimmed off of the milk. If they were lucky they may have a separator which was a devise that the milk was run through, thus separating the cream and milk. The pioneer that had a milk cow had ready sales of milk and cream to their neighbors.

At some point the milk and cream would sour. From the sour cream they would make butter. From the sour milk they also made cheese and cottage cheese.

Cheese consists chiefly of the pressed curd of milk. The characteristic flavor of cheese is due to the process of manufacture, the source of milk and the presence of bacteria and mold. There are many varieties of cheese.

Making Butter

Pour the sour cream (sweet may be used also) in a butter churn and start churning. The movement of the churn, be it the up and down motion or a churn with a paddle, causes the butter to form. Drain off the buttermilk. Place the butter in cold water and work and rinse until all of the buttermilk is washed out. Salt may be added and worked in. Mold and store in a cool place. Some households had butter molds in which the butter was packed to form a specific shape. Some molds had designs in them, thus making for very pretty molded butter. There were various styles of churns.

When the wagon trains were moving across the country a bucket with a tight cover was filled with cream and hung under the wagon. As the wagon moved across the plains, the bucket moved back and forth and at the end of the day they had their butter.

Brine for Butter Storage

If keeping butter for an extended period of time, make a brine to he
preserve it. Boil three gallons of water, ½ cup sugar and one tablespo
saltpeter with enough salt added to float an egg. When cold, strain throu
cloth. Wrap rolls of butter in cloth, place in a jar or crock, pour cold bri
over butter. Place a weight on the butter to keep butter under surface
brine. Store in cool place.

Longhorn Cheese

1 1/2 gallons thick clabbered milk
    (fresh milk, not homogenized)
4 tablespoons fresh butter
3/4 teaspoons soda
2/3 cup thick sour cream
1 1/4 teaspoons salt
1/4 teaspoon butter
Coloring

Be sure to have raw milk. Place on stove and cook for half an ho
stirring frequently to separate the curd from the whey. At the end
cooking, the curd will be very tough. Drain off the whey and press cur
under a heavy weight until the whey is all pressed out and curd is dr
Failure to do this will result in a poorly finished product. Add fresh butt
and soda to dry curd. Chop until curd is quite fine and ingredients a
thoroughly mixed. Press mixture down into bowl and let stand in a war
place for 2 1/2 hours. Then put cheese into double boiler with sour crear
salt and coloring. As it begins to heat, stir until all ingredients melt into
mass. Then pour it into a well-greased bowl and allow to cool; It is reac
to eat as soon as it is cold.

To cure the cheese, remove it from bowl, when cool and cover tl
whole surface with melted paraffin and store in a cool place.

This recipe makes about 1 1/2 pounds of cheese. – *Myrna (Shafe*
Carpita

Tip . . .

Clabbered milk is unpasteurized milk that is allowed to thicken &
curdle forming a sour flavor.

24

Cottage Cheese

Place pan of sour milk that has clabbered on back of stove. Don't let get too hot or it will be stringy and tough. When it is set, drain the whey ᵈd mix with cream, top with sugar. *Fresh, raw milk, not homogenized.

Curds and Cream

Place raw milk on stove, cook for half an hour, stirring until curds and hey are separated. Drain whey from curds but do not press curds. When ᵒol, serve with fresh, sweet cream, sugar and nutmeg if available.

Baked Custard

3 egg yolks
1 egg
Pinch of salt

1 pint milk
1/3 cup sugar

Beat egg yolks and egg, add sugar. Add milk and a pinch of salt. This ᵃn be baked in a pan by itself or it may be put in a pie shell. Bake in a ᵒoderate oven until firm in center.

When you want to caramel custard, than take 2/3 cup of granulated ᵤgar, melt the sugar until it turns a light brown and then add it to the ᵇiling milk.

Other spices and flavorings such as vanilla, nutmeg, cinnamon, etc. ᵃy also be added.

Pudding

1/3 cup flour
1/4 teaspoon salt
2 tablespoons butter
1/2 teaspoon vanilla

2/3 cup sugar
2 cups milk
3 egg yolks, beaten

Mix together the flour, sugar and salt. Gradually add milk. Cook over ᵒt water 10 to 15 minutes or until thick. Add butter and egg yolks, cook minutes longer. Cool and add vanilla.

This is a basic recipe. Various flavorings may be used, including ʰocolate. This may be served as pudding, topped with fruit or used as a ᵢe filling. Top with whipped cream and serve.

25

Corn Starch Pudding

THEN: 2 cups milk
                2 egg yolks or 1 whole egg - beaten
                1 cup sugar
                2 tablespoons corn starch

Bring milk to boil - add beaten egg yolks, sugar and cornstarch t have been mixed together. Cook till thickened. Pour into desert bowls a cool. Serve with cream if desired.

NOW: 2 cups milk
                1 box instant vanilla pudding mix

Combine milk and pudding mix, whip or shake till thick. - *Lou Shafer*

Making Ice Cream

Many a gallon of ice cream has been made with the hand cra freezer. Ice from the ice house was used or better yet, a snow dr was found in late summer, and snow was hauled home to use to freeze t ice cream.

The hand crank freezer consists of a wooden bucket, a metal contain with a lid, with an internal wooden paddle, and a cap/handle with ge that turns the metal container around and around. The custard, cream other ice cream makin's are placed in the metal container, the paddle in, the lid is put on the metal container and then it is placed down into t wooden bucket, fitting on a spindle. The handle apparatus is then fitted to the lid of the metal container. This leaves about an inch space betwe the metal container and the wooden bucket. Layers of ice and rock salt a

 alternated until the ice is packed around t edges of the bucket, but still allows the insi container to turn. The handle is turned, rotatir the inside container and interior paddle. Ro salt is added to the ice or snow to hasten t freezing process.

The handle is turned, the metal contain goes 'round and 'round and after a time the i cream is frozen and ready to eat.

Custard Ice Cream

2 eggs	1 teaspoon vanilla
2 cups milk-scalded	1/8 teaspoon salt
6 tablespoons sugar	1 1/2 cups cream

Beat eggs until yolks and whites are blended. Add sugar and salt. Mix well. Add milk slowly, stirring constantly. Cook over hot water until mixture coats a spoon. Remove from fire at once. Chill. Add flavoring and cream. Place in an ice cream freezer and freeze.

Strawberry Ice Cream

Whip stiff 1/2 gallon cream with 1 cup sugar. Add whites of 3 or 4 eggs whipped stiff and mixed with 1 cup sugar. Mash and strain through cheese cloth 3 boxes strawberries, sweetened thoroughly and add to the cream after it begins to freeze. Raspberries or other berries may be used also.

Ice Cream Cones

Ice cream cones came into being in the late 1800's and became popular with the general population at the 1904 St. Lewis World's Fair.

Roman Cream

Put 1/4 box of gelatin into 1 quart of milk; soak a little while, then add the beaten yolks of 2 eggs and 1 cup of sugar; cook for a few minutes, then add the beaten whites; cool and freeze. To give it a carmel flavor, scorch some of the sugar. - *The Peoples Home Recipe Book by Mrs. Alice G. Kirk, 1913*

Tutti Frutti

When vanilla ice cream is partially frozen add candied cherries, chopped citron, chopped raisins or other candied fruit chopped rather fine. Use about half the quantity of fruit that there is ice cream. - *The Peoples Home Recipe Book by Mrs. Alice G. Kirk, 1913*

Gathering Wood

Before you could cook on a wood stove or a camp fire you had to have wood. Now getting wood in the "good ole" days was far different from today. For starts they did not have the pickup truck to haul the wood with. They were lucky if they had a horse or better yet, a horse and wagon. Today the pickup truck is filled with gas, oil checked, chain saw thrown in the back and miles later down the road a favorite wood "gitt'n" spot is found. Now in the early days there were no chain saws or pickup trucks to ride in, nor roads to drive on. Maybe they had an ax and if real lucky a hand saw of some kind. The early settler looked to the nearest supply of wood. This may be on the nearby mountain, hill side or creek bottom. Sometimes they might take the horse to the hills and drag a log home to be sawed and cut up later. Better yet if they could get there with a wagon they could bring several logs home for a larger supply. Now, there were no tools or transportation to get the wood then this meant you had to find wood that was small enough to break up by your own shear strength. The smaller wood was found in the willow patches near the creek or sage brush was burned. Any way you look at it, the wood had to be gathered and sawed or broken to the proper length for the stove or camp fire. Also you had to have small pieces of wood to start your fire. This may be small branches that were gathered or blocks of wood that was cut into very thin pieces

and is called "kindling". If "pitch" wood could be found, then that made for easier fire building. "Pitch" wood is wood that the pitch from the pine tree has accumulated in large amounts and burns very easily and creates quick, hot fire.

Wood gathering was generally done in the summer and fall so as to have enough wood stored for cooking and for warmth in the long, cold winter months.

Wood actually produces warmth four times; when you go get it, when you saw and chop it up, when you haul it in and when you burn it.
Myrna (Shafer) Carpita

DESSERTS

Food for Angels

By Jeanette Stevenson

The other day I sat in with a group of women who were planning a church dinner. When the question of dessert came up, the unanimous favorite was angel food cake with strawberries and whipped cream, "It is so easy to make and so easy to serve."

As I listened to the comments on whether Betty Crocker or Duncan Hines put out the best box of Angel food mix, it occurred to me that the progression of making an angel food from the homesteader days until the present was really part of the history of Montana.

To begin with, in those early days as a homesteader's kid down in Powder River country more years ago than I like to recall, angel food cake was usually a summer dessert. Chickens quit laying in the winter and although coaxed with hot water and cooked scraps only reluctantly shelled out enough eggs for dire necessity. Never a whole dozen to spare - which was what it took for a cake. However, in the spring when the first green grass came and the hens could go out of the coop without freezing their combs and their feet, everyone said, "Any old feather duster would lay", and so angel food once again graced the table for birthdays and other special occasions.

Of course, that was only the beginning. I can remember my mother telling a neighbor that the eggs must not be too old or too fresh and not too cold or too warm. Usually there was no cake flour, so another topic was how much corn starch to add to the cup of flour. Also, could a hand beater be used or was a wire whip necessary? And how big a bowl? Some women used a big platter.

After all the sifting, the measuring, the careful separating of the eggs (heaven help you if a speck of the yolk went into the mixture), and after all the whipping, the folding, finally the heavenly mixture was placed in the pan.

And now came another crucial, perhaps the most crucial, part of the while process. Those old coal and wood stoves were tricky individuals, each with its own perverse quirks. The heat for baking was very important. A shade too hot and the eggs would not expand properly, too cool and the batter would not cook. Of course, there were no thermometers on those stoves, but who needed one? Any cook could tell

29

the right temperature for cake, meat or pie by merely putting her hand the oven. Some put the cake in a cold oven and then built a fire ve slowly and tended it carefully. I remember my mother-in-law, who w from Missouri, saying that they always used corn cobs. She could tell y the exact number it took.

While the cake was in the oven, all activity ceased in the kitche Children were banned, and shooed outside, "You might make the ca fall." And woe to a husband who came in and slammed the screen door.

After the best part of an hour, the cook carefully peeked in. Anoth decision: was it done? Well, maybe another minute. Where is a broc straw to stick in it and test it? If taken out too soon and inverted over a bottle, usually the catsup bottle, the cake would collapse and fall out of the pan.

Carefully loosened, frosted and placed on a special cake plate, it was ready to be admired and eventually served, perhaps for a special dinner or a meeting of the women's sewing circle, at a community dance in the school house, or at a neighbor's threshing. One seldom had angle food at the home threshing - too much would be going on in the kitchen and too many things had to go in the oven. But whenever it was served, the oohs and aahs that greeted it were ample reward for all the effort.

Mother's Wish?

"O, weary mothers mixing dough,
Don't you wish that food would grow?
Your lips would smile I know to see
A cookie bush or a pancake tree."

- *The Peoples Home Recipe Book by Mrs. Alice G. Kirk, 1913*

CAKES

Angel Food Cake

HEN:

1 cup egg whites - 8-10 eggs
1 1/4 cups sugar
1 cup cake flour
1 teaspoon cream of tarter

1/2 teaspoon salt
1/2 teaspoon vanilla
1 tablespoon water

Sift flour and sugar separately 4 times. Measure each after first
ﬁfting. Whip egg whites lightly with an egg beater. Add salt, water and
avorings when half beaten. Sift in cream of tartar. Continue whipping
ﬁtil whites hold their shape. Divide sugar into fourths. Fold in each
ﬁurth with 10 careful strokes of the spatula. Divide flour into fourths.
ﬁld in each fourth with 10 careful strokes of the spatula. Pour into
ﬁoiled tube pan. Bake in slow oven (325° F.) for 50 minutes.
   Mixed by hand using "elbow grease".

OW: Today get a boxed cake mix and mix with your mixer. You don't
ﬁen have to separate the eggs or build a fire in the old wood range. Just
ﬁrn a switch and twist a dial to the desired temperature. Now there is
ﬁen a timer to tell you when it is done. - *Louise Shafer*

Angel Cake

1 cup cake flour
3/4 cup sugar
1 3/4 cups egg whites
3/4 teaspoons salt
1 1/2 teaspoons cream of tartar
3/4 cup sugar
1 teaspoon vanilla extract

Sift flour with 3/4 cups sugar four times. Beat egg whites with salt until
ﬁothy; add cream of tartar and beat until stiff but not dry. Add remaining
ﬁ4 cup sugar, 1 tablespoon at a time, folding in thoroughly. Add vanilla
ﬁxtract with last addition of sugar. Sift flour mixture over top, a little at a
ﬁme, and fold in lightly with a down-up-over motion. Bake in 10 inch
ﬁngreased angel cake pan in moderate oven (325°) for 75 minutes. Invert
ﬁan to cool.

31

Stoning Raisins

In the early days all grapes had seeds in them. When the grapes w dried into raisins the seeds were left in them. The cook had to prepa the raisins by "stoning" them. In order to do this the raisins were placed warm water to soften and then taken out, one by one, and rubbed betwe the fingers and thumb to remove the seeds. After this process v completed the raisins were used as called for in a receipt. Other fruits t were dried with the seeds or pits in also had to be "stoned".

To Make Cake Flour

For every cup of flour, remove 2 tablespoons of flour, now add tablespoons corn starch to every cup of flour, sift 5- 6 times.

Apple Sauce Cake

1 cup sugar	1/4 pound butter
2 eggs	1 teaspoon cinnamon
1/2 teaspoon nutmeg	2 cups flour
1 cup apple sauce	1 teaspoon soda in apple sauce
1/2 teaspoon salt	1 cup raisins

Cream sugar and butter, add eggs and mix thoroughly. Sift together of your dry ingredients. Add dry ingredients alternately with the app sauce/soda mixture. Fold in raisins. Pour into a loaf pan. Bake 45 minut at 350°.

Again, if mixed by hand this requires a lot of "elbow grease".

Gold Cake

3 tablespoons shortening	3/4 cup sugar
3 egg yolks	3 teaspoons baking powder
1/2 cup milk	1 1/2 cups flour
1 teaspoon flavoring	

Cream shortening; add sugar slowly; add egg yolks which have be beaten until thick; add flavoring. Sift together flour and baking powd add alternately, with milk to first mixture. Bake in greased loaf pan 375° for 35 minutes.

One-Egg Cake

2/3 cup sugar
1/4 cup shortening
1/4 teaspoon salt
1 teaspoon vanilla

1 egg
1 1/2 cups flour
1/2 cup milk
2 teaspoons baking powder

Cream shortening and sugar. Add unbeaten egg. Add flavoring, beat thoroughly. Sift flour, measure and sift with salt and baking-powder. Add alternately with milk to creamed shortening and sugar. Pour into well oiled loaf pan. Bake in moderate oven (375°) 35 minutes.

Try one of these sometime, all by hand. It sure will build hand and arm muscles and also shows you how weak we have become.

NOW: Either buy a boxed cake mix and mix according to the instructions or go the bakery section of your store and buy the cake ready-made. - *Louise Shafer*

Measure for Measure Cake

2, 3, 4, or 5 eggs
cake flour (same measure as eggs)
sugar (same measure as eggs)
dash of salt for each egg
1/8 teaspoon cream of tartar for each egg
1/4 teaspoon vanilla for each egg

Break eggs into glass. Measure an equal amount of flour and sugar. Place eggs in mixing bowl with salt, cream of tartar, flavoring and about 1/4 of sugar. Beat until very thick and light colored. Beat at least 1 minute for each egg. Add rest of sugar gradually. Add flour all at once and stir in quickly and thoroughly. Bake in ungreased angel food cake pan 30 to 45 minutes. - *Louise Shafer*

Sourdough Raisin Cake

3 cups milk	1 cup sourdough starter
2 cups brown sugar	2 cups flour

Combine the above ingredients and let stand over night.

2 cups butter	1/4 teaspoon nutmeg
1/2 cup sugar	3 eggs
2 teaspoons cinnamon	1 teaspoon soda
1 pound raisins	1 gill brandy

In the morning cream shortening and sugar. Add eggs, mi thoroughly. Add sourdough mixture, spices, raisins and brandy. Be thoroughly. Butter and flour cake pans. Let stand in pans and rise about a hour. Bake at 375° for 35 minutes.

Devil's Cake

For the custard part - one cup each grated chocolate and brown suga 1/2 cup sweet milk, 1 yolk of egg, 1 teaspoon vanilla. Stir all together an cook slowly and let cool. For cake part - One cup brown sugar, 1/2 cu butter, 2 1/2 cups flour, 1/2 cup sweet milk, 2 eggs, 1 teaspoon soda. Fc frosting - 2 cups white sugar, 1 cup water, 1 tablespoon vinegar. Boil unt thick like candy and stir in the beaten whites of 2 eggs and 1/3 pound c marshmallows. Boil again and place on cake. - *Iris Gleed*

Jelly Roll

Four eggs, beaten light, 4 tablespoons of sugar, 5 tablespoons c flour, 1 tablespoon of water, and a pinch of salt, beat light. Bake in square tin in a quick oven. Turn out on a tea towel, spread with jelly an roll.

Pure Baking Powder

Mix together 2 pounds of pure cream of tartar, one pound of bakin soda, 1/2 pound of corn starch, and 1/2 pound of flour. Sift 7 or 8 time through a fine sieve.

Cream of Tartar

From rich, ripe, luscious grapes comes cream of tartar - the precious ingredient of the best baking powder.

In the world's most famous vineyards the grapes are picked - their juice gently pressed out and set aside to cool and age. In the juice the wonderful process of Cream of Tartar crystallization takes place. These crystals go through a rigorous process of refinement, which includes many washings in boiling water and re-crystallization, and at last are groomed into a very fine white powder. The great care taken throughout results in a product of remarkable purity.

Only a few generations ago there was no prepared baking powder as we know it today; your grandmother used cream of tartar and soda to make her delicious cakes and biscuits rise.

And cream of tartar is still the best ingredient known for baking powder. It makes a thoroughly reliable baking powder that leavens as well for a beginner as for an experienced cook. It makes a thoroughly wholesome baking powder because it is a pure product of ripe grapes.

Knitting

Need socks? Need hats? Need gloves? Oh, and how about a sweater? Yes, most women in the pioneer days were very proficient in the skill of knitting. They kept their family in a good supply of socks, and stockings, gloves or mittens and stocking hats and other knit items. A lot of women never set down without knitting. If they had a large family this was a very big and important job to be done.

Many women in the early day made their own yarn with fiber gleaned from their own herds of sheep and some grew flax and processed the fiber into thread and yarn. The materials were gathered throughout the year and kept for the long winter days to be cleaned, carded and spun into thread and yarn. Then they knit what was needed for their family and friends. In later years yarn and thread could be purchased and helped reduce the work of the housewife.

"Darn" That Hole

As knit socks, mittens or gloves wore out they were not thrown aw
and another one bought as we do today. They were repaired and t
was called "darning". The process of darning was to select the prop
color and size of thread or yarn to match the item that is to be repaired.
"darning egg" or any smooth, round, hard object is inserted in the soc
This enables the sock to be stretched to the proper shape and size a
 allows for easier "darning". The thread
woven around the area to be darned and th
back and forth across the hole, weaving t
thread to form a patch. Done properly there
very little difference in the patched area and t
original knit article.

How Did the Clothing Get That Color?

The lady of the house not only made her own yarns for knitting a
weaving but also dyed them in very pleasing colors. Colors for t
yarns were made from many different things. Various plants creat
different colors as did various minerals and chemicals. There we
different methods of dyeing for wool, cotton and linen. A small sample
how this was done is as follows:

Yellow - for Cotton – For 5 pounds of goods dissolve 1 pound of sug
of lead in enough water to thoroughly wet the goods and in the san
quantity of water in another vessel dissolve 1/2 pound of bi-chromate
potash. Dip goods well and drain in each alternately until of the desir
shade, then rinse and hang up to dry.

Yellow – for Wool – For 5 pounds of goods make a solution by adding
ounces of alum and 3 ounces of bi-chromate of potash to enough water
color the goods and boil them in this for half an hour; lift and air un
well cooled and drained, then work for half an hour in a bath with
pounds of fustic. Wash and hang up to dry. . - *The Peoples Home Recip
Book by Mrs. Alice G. Kirk, 1913*

This is just a sample of what was used to dye fabric. Solutions cou
be made for most all colors at home as needed as there were not premac
dyes as are found in stores today.

COOKIES

Sugar Cookies

1 cup butter or lard
1 cup sugar
2 eggs (3 if small)
1 tablespoon water
1 teaspoon vanilla
1 teaspoon baking powder
3/4 teaspoon salt
3 cups flour (about)

Cream shortening and sugar, add eggs and water and mix well. Add ry ingredients and mix well. Roll out and cut. Bake at 375° for about 8 inutes.
Try rolling out cookies with a beer bottle, a length of broom or shovel andle. This might be all that they had available at times. Not all of the ld timers had rolling pins and they used whatever was handy. - *Louise hafer*

Macaroons

1/2 pound sugar   1/2 pound almonds
3 whites of egg

Beat the whites of eggs to a snow white and mix well with sugar. Then dd almonds, blanched and grated and should the paste be too moist add a w dry bread crumbs. Place in little heaps on a buttered tin and bake to ale brown. - *A Cook Book Containing Recipes of Quality – 1912*

Shortbread

1/2 pound butter   1/2 cup powdered sugar
2 cups flour   pinch of salt

Mix butter and sugar together, add flour. Make balls and press with ork. Bake. - *Louise Shafer*

Oatmeal Cookies

One and one-half cups flour, 1 1/2 cups rolled oats, 1 1/4 cups bro(w)
sugar, 3/4 cup butter, 1 teaspoon soda. More flour may be added. Rol(l)
double with boiled dates between, cut in squares. Bake.

Ginger Creams

2 cups sugar	1/2 teaspoon salt
2 cups sour cream	1 teaspoon ginger
4 eggs	1 teaspoon cinnamon
1 cup molasses	6 cups flour
4 level teaspoons soda	

Mix well. Drop from spoon. (The old recipe did not call for frosti(ng)
but I frost with powdered sugar, milk and vanilla) - *Louise Shafer*

Soft Cookies

1 cup sugar
1 egg beaten light
1/2 cup butter or lard
1/2 cup sour milk
1 teaspoon soda, nutmeg & vanilla
flour to make dough

"I found this in the Comfort Magazine in
1896 or about. All who have used it since have
liked it." - Grandma Hand *[Maggie]* - *Reprint
with permission, copyrighted-1992, MAGGIE
by Myrna (Shafer) Carpita*

Sour Cream Cookies

One cup sour cream, 1/2 cup butter, 1 cup sugar, 3 eggs, 1 teaspo(on)
vanilla, 1 teaspoon lemon, heaping teaspoon baking powder, 1/4 teaspo(on)
soda in cream, flour enough for soft dough. Roll out, sprinkle with sug(ar)
cut and bake in quick oven.

PIES

Pie Crust

4 cups flour   1 teaspoon salt
1 3/4 cups lard*   1/2 cup cold water

Cut lard into flour and salt to a good crumb stage. Add water; if too dry add a little more water. Makes two full 9" crusts and one shell. *You can use part lard and part rendered chicken fat. - *Louise Shafer*

Tip . . .

When baking a single pie crust you can prevent the crust from blistering if you prick crust with a fork and set another empty pie tin over the crust when you put it in the oven to bake.

Vinegar Pie

1 cup water   1 cup sugar
1/2 cup flour   3 tablespoons vinegar
pinch of salt   butter - size of an egg
a little nutmeg

Stir all together and boil. When it becomes thick, pour into baked pie shell. Serve with whipped cream. Tastes like lemon pie. - *Louise Shafer*

Rhubarb or Wild Gooseberry Pie

3 cups rhubarb (cut 1/2" pieces)   4 tablespoons flour
    or gooseberries   2 tablespoons butter
1 1/2 cups sugar

Place fruit in crust lined pan. Mix sugar and flour together; pour over fruit in pie tin. Dot with butter. Cover with top crust and pinch together to keep the juice in. If the bottom crust is moistened around the edge of pan it will stick together better. - *Louise Shafer*

39

Buttermilk Pie

Yolk of 4 eggs, 1 cup sugar, 2 cups fresh buttermilk, 1 tablespoo butter rolled in 2 tablespoons flour. Flavor with nutmeg and bake in a ric crust. Add a meringue made of the whites of the eggs and sugar.

Carrot Pie

Two medium carrots grated and cooked in a little milk, then 2 egg well beaten, 1 teaspoon ginger and cinnamon each, 1/2 cup sugar, 1 cu milk. Bake in 1 crust.- *Reprint with permission, copyrighted -199 MAGGIE, by Myrna (Shafer) Carpita*

Green Apple Pie

Peel, core and slice tart apples into a bowl. Add 3 tablespoons or t taste of sugar, cinnamon to taste and about a tablespoon of flour fc thickening. Mix well. Place mixture in a pie pan that has been lined with pie crust. Sprinkle a few drops of water and add a few bits of butter. To with a pie crust, seal. Bake at 375° to 400°, depending on oven for abou 40 minutes or until bubbly in the center.

Rhubarb or Pie Plant

Rhubarb was found in many pioneer gardens. The root "starts" wer probably brought with the pioneers on their move west and then share with others. Rhubarb was a favorite as it is an early spring plant. It is perennial plant and grows well in the Montana climate. The large lea stalks were pulled when harvested with the large leaves being cut o immediately to avoid wilting. Rhubarb makes wonderful pies, either b itself or mixed with other fruits, wine and sauces.

Huckleberry Pie

Clean a quart of huckleberries. Take off stems and remove unrip berries. Place in bowl. Add 1/2 to 3/4 cup sugar and a tablespoon of flou Mix lightly. Place berries into a crust lined pie pan. Place a top crust ove the berries and seal. Cut holes in the top of the crust to vent steam. Bak for about 40 to 60 minutes.

Tip . . .

weet potatoes and various types of squash were also used for pies
nd made similar to the Pumpkin Pie.

Pumpkin or Squash Pie

Cut a ripe pumpkin or squash in half, remove seeds and peal hide off.
ut into chunks and place in a pan with a little water. Cook slowly until
ery tender, drain off water. Run the pulp through a colander or mash to a
ne pulp.
   If you prefer, you can prepare the pumpkin or squash but do not peal.
lace the pieces on tins and set them in the oven. Bake slowly until done.
crape the pulp and run through a colander or mash to a fine pulp.

1 quart milk	4 eggs, beaten
3 cups pumpkin or squash pulp	salt (a pinch)
1/2 cup sugar	ginger, to taste
1/2 cup molasses	cinnamon, to taste

   Beat all together. Line pie tins with a pie crust, flute sides, pour in the
ie mixture. Bake at 375° approximately 1 hour or until a knife inserted in
enter of pie comes out clean. Makes three pies.

   Maggie Hand, Louise Shafer's
randmother, wrote about pumpkins:
With the scarcity of fruits these lowly
egetables filled a much wanted need
vhich I think lead to a winter pie filling
alled Pumpkin Leather. Pumpkins were
ooked and ran thru a sieve. Then about the
ame quantity of sorghum molasses added,
oiled and stirred till thick, spread on plates and put out to dry in the sun,
p high away from cats, dogs or children. Taken in nights and replaced
gain in the sun till dry, put in a paper sack if possible (these commodities
vere scarce) and hung on the ridge log for pies. When soaked up in milk,
n egg added, poured in a pie shell and baked, made a good pie. Mother
ried to dry pumpkin leather but she had too many hungry, growing girls
o ever get it into a pie. - *Reprint with permission, copyrighted -1992
MAGGIE, by Myrna (Shafer) Carpita*

41

Pumpkin Leather

Cook your pumpkin, put through a sieve and then taking 1 3/4 cup the pumpkin pulp add 1/4 cup white sugar, boil together and then spre on cookie sheets and place in an oven, food dryer or in the hot sun to dry
There will be a loss of approximately 1/2 of the bulk of the pulp due evaporation of the liquid. It takes quite a while to dry but when do makes excellent fruit leather. Store in a dry cool place. When ready make a pie, follow the pie recipe.

Pumpkin Leather makes excellent pies. I did not use the molasses Maggie (Halbert) Hand stated her mother did. I do not like the flavor molasses, but molasses may be substituted for the sugar. -Myrna Carpit **Reprint with permission, copyrighted -1992 MAGGIE, by Myr. (Shafer) Carpita**

Pumpkin Pie (in a sack)

The night before you wish to bake your pie, tear pumpkin leather in small pieces, place in a bowl, add 1 1/4 cup water and one can evaporat milk, cover, place in fridge. Next day, stir until all pumpkin leather dissolved. Add the following:

3/4 cup brown sugar	3/4 teaspoon ginger
2 eggs, beaten	1/4 teaspoon ground cloves
1 teaspoon cinnamon	1/2 teaspoon salt
1 teaspoon nutmeg	

Mix thoroughly, pour into unbaked pie shell. Bake at 400° f approximately 40 minutes or until a knife inserted in pie comes out clea -Myrna Carpita - **Reprint with permission, copyrighted -1992 MAGGL by Myrna (Shafer) Carpita**

OTHER GOODIES

Bread Pudding

1 cup bread cubes
1 egg, slightly beaten
1/4 cup sugar
1/2 cup raisins

1/4 teaspoon salt
1/2 teaspoon cinnamon
2 cups milk, scalded

Combine sugar, cinnamon, salt, milk and egg. Add bread cubes and
raisins, mix thoroughly. Pour into well buttered baking dish. Bake at 350°
for about 1 hour. Cool, serve with cream.

Carrot Pudding
(A Christmas Favorite)

1 cup brown sugar
1 cup seedless raisins
1 cup currants
1 cup grated carrots
1 cup nuts
1 1/2 cups flour

1 teaspoon nutmeg
1 teaspoon cinnamon
1 teaspoon soda
1 teaspoon salt
1/4 cup cold water
1 egg beaten

Mix together put in cheese cloth, can or mold. Steam for 3 hours.

Old Fashioned Strawberry Shortcake

2 cups flour
2 tablespoons sugar
3 tablespoons shortening

1/2 teaspoon salt
4 teaspoons baking power
3/4 cup milk
1 quart berries

Sift dry ingredients; mix in shortening; add milk to
make soft dough, smooth out lightly. Bake in greased
cake tin at 475° for 20 to 25 minutes. Split, cover
with berries and a bit of whipped cream.

43

Tip . . .

If you wash strawberries thoroughly before stemming there will be waste and your berries will stay firm.

Biscuit Cobbler

This particular cobbler is made with rhubarb but any fruit may used.

3 cups diced rhubarb	1 cup sugar
2 tablespoons flour	1/2 cup water

Wash and dice rhubarb, put in greased baking dish with water. M flour and sugar and sprinkle over rhubarb. Dot with butter.

1 cup flour	1/4 teaspoon salt
1 teaspoon baking powder	4 tablespoons of butter
1/2 cup milk	

Sift dry ingredients together. Cut in butter and add milk, mix to ma dough. Drop by spoons full on top of rhubarb mixture and bake at 35 for 30 minutes.

Raspberry Flummery

Flummeries were fruit puddings made with blackberries, raspberri strawberries or gooseberries. They were among the pastries and desse that appeared on the table at the end of an elegant dinner.

2 cups berries	1/2 teaspoon salt
1/2 cup cold water	4 tablespoons cornstarch
1/2 cup sugar or to taste	

Put berries in a pan with 1/2 cup water. Cook until soft. Mix oth ingredients and slowly add to berries, stirring. Cook until mixtu thickens. Spoon into glasses - serve chilled.

Cream Puffs

Put 1/2 cup butter and 1 cup water over the fire. When boiling, add hastily 1 cupful of flour; stir until smooth. Take from the fire and when cool break in 1 egg, beat well then add a second egg; beat and add a third egg. Beat until smooth and light. Drop by tablespoonsful into gem tins, and bake in a moderate oven for about half an hour. Fill with custard, pudding or whipped cream.

Kitchen Cupboard

This is an example of the kitchen cupboard that the early pioneer woman might have been lucky enough to have. This was storage and work area combined and was probably, with exception of a table, the only work area that was available in her kitchen.

Most cupboards had bins for flour and maybe one for sugar. They were generally lined with tin. This helped to keep varmints out and kept everything clean. Some also had bread storage which was also lined with tin.

There were storage areas for your everyday dishes, bowls and cooking utensils, a shelf for pots and pans and in some cupboards there were even spice racks. There were also drawers for the silverware and other items.

The work area in some cupboards could be pulled out giving extra work space but put back when one was finished working.

There were various designs and types of cupboards available. All in all the cupboards contained just about everything that was used in the kitchen. The kitchens in most pioneer homes were generally small and also served as the dining room.

45

Putting Up Ice

Winter was a time to put up ice. Put up ice, you say? How did the do that?

The creeks and ponds were frozen and large blocks of ice about 2 fe square were cut with the same saws that wood was sawed with, althoug some folks had regular ice saws. The ice w then hauled from the creek and put in a ho that had been dug in the ground, a wel insulated building or whatever was availab so it could be covered with sawdust, ha straw or old blankets to keep it cold. This ic would then keep most of the summer an provided for at least some refrigeration keep foodstuffs cool and of course, make ice cream if you were luck enough to have an ice cream freezer.

Ice Tongs

Some people had ice boxes (same as a refrigerator, just not electri that they put ice in to keep food cool.

How did they pick up the ice and pack it around? They used ic tongs, if they had them. These tongs allowed the ice to be picked u without touching the ice and freezing your hands. Although on a hot summer day packing ice around might not have been a bad job.

If a small piece of ice was wanted, then there generally was an ice pick available to break off the chunk of ice.

Ice Pick

Tip . . .

Cleaning Wallpaper – dust the walls first with a feather duster. Ru the wallpaper with a stale piece of bread, beginning at top an drawing to the bottom of the wall. To remove a grease spot, place a absorbent paper or felt material over the spot and apply a hot iron o paper or cloth.

MEATS

Meat Storage and Preservation

At the time Bannack, Virginia City, Argenta and other surrounding areas were rip roarin' the preservation of meat presented a very large problem in comparison to today. There was no refrigeration, except during the winter and you just stepped out the door for plenty of it. Summertime was an entirely different situation and the pioneers had to provide a way to keep their food cold. They used stored ice but this was still limited refrigeration so they used other methods of preservation.

Meat Preservation

In the very early pioneer days, before the pioneers settled and could raise animals, the wild game was their main supply of meat. As pioneers began to raise animals it was easier to butcher. The beef or domestic animals were shot, then raised on a tripod with a block and tackle, gutted, skinned and cooled.

In the summer, during the day time, meat was covered and laid on top of the ice to keep it cool and then at night the meat was hung high on a tripod or tree so it would air. In the morning it was taken down, cut off what was needed for the day and put back on the ice. Beef and wild meat was mostly eaten fresh during the summer. In the winter the meat was simply hung outside and used as needed. If the meat was to be preserved for any amount of time there were several ways of doing this. Salting, smoking, pickling, drying (jerking) and placing meats in lard (meat potting) were methods that not only preserved the food, but added flavor also. - *Louise Shafer*

The Whole Animal Was Used

All parts of the animal were eaten or used in some manner. The brain, kidney, tongue, tripe, heart, liver were cooked and eaten. The fat was rendered and had many uses in a pioneer household. The intestines were cleaned and saved to use as casings for sausages. Sinew was also saved from the animal and was used to sew with.

Sausage making was another method of meat preservation. Meat was ground, spices and salt added, stuffed into the casings, smoked and hung in a cool dry place for later use.

Pioneer meat preservation methods are still used today but the convenience of refrigeration and freezing is unsurpassed.

47

Jerky

THEN: In a crock or glass container, fill about half full with water; a enough salt until a fresh egg will float in the brine. Cut your meat - be venison, elk - about 1 inch thick and 6 to 8 inches long. Place meat brine. Let stand in brine for about two weeks, occasionally rearrangi meat and stirring.

Drain brine off meat, wash in cold water. You can either hang t meat over wires or place in a smoker and smoke until dry. Store in an tight container.

NOW: Take a drive down to your nearest gas station/convenience sto and displayed by the cash register you will find packages of jerky in variety of shapes and sizes along with flavors from "original", "ho "extra hot" teriyaki", "honey cured" and probably a new and bet version of jerky that was added to the display just before you walked Buy it, open package and chew to your hearts content!

How to use Jerky

Shred jerky, place in container and pour hot water over jerky. L stand in water about an hour, drain. Add to cream gravy and serve ov toast, add to stews or any other dish you might want meat in.

Meat Drying

Drying meat, a preservation method, was also done, but witho placing the meat in salt brine. This was a primary meat preservatic method used by the American Indians. The meat is cut one forth to thr eights inch thick and then placed on drying frames, on clothes lines, c sheets, over brush or any other surface that allows the air to circula around the meat and allows it to be placed in the sun to dry. The me might also be placed over a low burning fire in order to speed the dryir process and discourage any insects that might want to share in the bount The primary goal is to remove all moisture from the meat and then i bacteria can grow and spoil it. This meat could easily be stored in bags baskets that are sealed and placed where animals and insects cannot reac it.

Jerky and dried meat also traveled well. With the moisture removed made it weigh less and also could be eaten just as is or cooked in stew soups, etc.

Salting Meat

All meat can be salted as a method of preservation but pork is
primarily used, thus the term "salt pork". Pieces of the butchered pig,
weighing 10 to 15 pounds, are placed in a barrel or crock with a salt brine
salt being packed between each piece of meat so the meat does not
touch. The meat remains in the salt or salt brine for up to a week. The
meat is then removed from the barrel, making sure the salt has soaked
completely through the meat, dried off and placed in a cloth sack and
hung in a cool place. This will last up to six weeks without spoiling. In
order to keep the meat even longer it may be smoked for three or four
days. Smoked meat not only lasts up to three or four months, the smoking
process gives an excellent flavor as well.

When meat is soaked in a salt brine the salt dehydrates or removes the
water and kills the bacteria that causes the meat to spoil. Smoking
dehydrates the meat even more, thus longer preservation.

Meat Potting or Placing in Lard

Meat potting can be used with any type of meat. It requires large
quantities of lard or rendered fat. A large crock is washed and scalded. A
layer of very hot fat is poured into the bottom of the crock. The animal is
butchered and cut up. The meat is then fried to very well done in fat. As
each piece of meat is cooked, it is placed in the crock on the fat, the meat
not touching the sides of the crock and then more fat is poured over the
meat until the meat is completely covered with the fat and sealed. This
cooking, and layering process is continued until the crock is filled. The
last couple of inches of the crock is filled with hot fat, thus sealing the
meat in. The crock is then covered with a lid, cloth or leather and put in a
cool place for keeping.

As the meat was needed for a meal it was taken out of the crock and
placed in the frying pan and cooked. When the meat was done, the very
hot fat was poured back into the crock to seal the remaining meat. Meat
could be kept up to six weeks with this method although if even a small
piece of meat was not completely cooked, it could spoil the whole batch.
Given our present methods of preserving meat, this is not the most
desirable method of meat preservation.

Tip . . .

To tenderize wild meat - soak overnight in vinegar. Rinse a prepare.

Pickling Meat

Pickling meat is done with a variety of recipes using vinegar a various spices. The meat is cooked in the vinegar solution and allowed soak in this solution for several days before using. The cooking of meat and the addition of vinegar kills the bacteria and preserves the m for a short time and gave it its own special flavor.

Wild Meat

When the prospectors came west in the gold rush there was not a of cattle or other domestic animals available for food. Therefore th relied on what they could glean from the land. A few of the men w came brought their families with them and they may also have brought a milk cow and maybe some chickens. Mainly they lived off of the deer, elk, moose, bear, birds and fish or other animals that could be gotten.

Tip . . .

To remove wild taste - use some vinegar, soda and salt. Soak me overnight. Rinse and prepare.

Roast Venison

Wash in warm water and dry well with a cloth. Salt and pepper taste. Place several strips of bacon over roast. Place in a covered roast with a little water, roast 3 to 4 hours. The last 30 minutes, uncover a continue to roast and allow to brown. Serve with a gravy made from own drippings. Carrots and potatoes may also be added the last hour cooking.

50

Venison Stew

Place 2 cups of cubed venison in a pan with bacon grease. Braise until brown on all sides, add water to cover, salt to taste. Cook meat until tender. Add onions, potatoes, carrots and more salt and pepper to taste. Add more water if necessary. Continue to cook until vegetables are done. The broth may be thickened by adding a little flour mixed with water or add dumplings the last few minutes of cooking.

Other meats may also be used such as elk, beef, or antelope. Also you may add other vegetables as you might have on hand.

Venison or Elk Steak

Cut thin, salt, pepper and flour it. Cook in hot grease until well done.

Wild Ducks

Before roasting, parboil them with a small peeled carrot, placed within each duck. This absorbs the unpleasant taste. An onion will have the same effect, but if onions are not liked, the carrot is better. Cook until tender, then roast 20 minutes, with or without dressing.

Sage Hen

Parboil in salt water with a little sage until tender, then place in the roaster, flour the fowl and lay thin slices of bacon on and around it. Make dressing the same as for turkey and stuff.

Fried Rabbit

Cut a cottontail in pieces to fry. Roll in flour, add salt and pepper and fry in butter until brown. Add about 2 cups of water and a scant half cup vinegar and allow to simmer from 1 to 1 1/2 hours. Remove meat and thicken the gravy with flour.

Some people prefer to parboil rabbits 10 minutes before frying. - *Recipes From Many Lands, N.D. Homemaker's Club – date unknown*

Trout

Dress and roll in flour. Fry in lard or bacon grease until brown. Season to taste.

Whitefish - Boiled

Fillet a large whitefish. Place in boiling, salted water and boil un[...] meat flakes. Remove from water, drain. Serve with butter for dipping.

Smoked Trout

Dress and clean well. If large trout, split down the back in two piece[...] Place the trout in a crock of salt brine. You may add other spices if yo[...] would like. Let soak for a couple of days.
Remove from brine, rinse. Place the trout
in a smoker. Build a low fire and add green
and dry wood as to create a smudge that is
allowed to "smoke" over the fish. Smoke
until fish are "dry" or to your taste. Store in cool place.

Pigeons

Many homesteaders had pigeon boxes in their barns, top of granari[...] or various other outbuildings. These consisted of a series of box[...] that the pigeons could nest in that had openings to the outside. On th[...] inside of the building there were doors that could b[...] opened to get to the nests. As the young grew to ne[...] maturity but before they could fly they were harvested. [...] young pigeon is known as a squab.

Tip . . .

If pigeon's legs are thin and the breast meat is dark, it is an indicatio[...] they are old and will probably be tough.

Broiled Squab

Remover feathers from squab, dress. Wash thoroughly. Split dow[...] center of back, flatten. Rub with salt, pepper and melted butter. Bro[...] under hot flame, turning until tender. If desired, strips of bacon may b[...] laid across breast of squab while broiling.

Tip . . .

Young pigeons will have light red breast meat and full flesh colore[...] legs.

Chickens

Did you ever stop and think of how we cook today in comparison to how the same foods prepared in the early times of Bannack, Virginia City and other early day settlements? For instance, did you know that for many years poultry could not be sold in or to a store or butcher shop if the head and entrails were removed? They were killed for sale to stores by sticking a sharp knife either under the eye or through the roof of the mouth into the brain.

In those days many homes had a few chickens, pigs and a cow in their back yards for meat, milk, butter and eggs. So all had to be prepared from scratch" so to speak. If the chicken was bought at the butcher shop or gotten from the back yard the cook had to prepare it for cooking. Most chickens were boiled as frying chickens could only be bought in the spring and summer. Baby chicks were hatched from eggs the hens laid and set on to incubate for 28 days and then raised to be killed as fryers or kept for the next year's crop. Fryers were, of course, the young tender chickens and were generally fried. The chickens that were boiled were generally the older hens and were usually tough so boiling was the general preparation for them. Once boiled the broth and meat was used for soup, chicken and noodles or chicken and dumplings. There was no refrigeration or freezers so they were killed as needed.

To prepare a chicken at home it had to be killed, most of the time by chopping its head off or winging its neck, then immersed in hot water, "scalded", so the feathers could be removed, then singed to get rid of the hairs that did not come off with the feathers. It was then washed to remove dirt the chicken had dusted in to keep its body free of parasites as well as cleaning its feathers, then "drawn" or entrails removed, rinsed and cut to serving sizes and prepared for dinner. - *Louise Shafer*

Cooked Eggs without Boiling

First put some boiling water into a large bowl or basin and let remain for a few seconds, then turn it out, lay in a couple of eggs and r͏ them over to take off the chill that they may not crack on application heat. Pour in upon the eggs boiling water from the kettle until they ͏ completely covered. Put a plate over them instantly and let them rem͏ upon the table for twelve minutes when they will be perfectly cooked, fr from all flavor of rawness and yet so delicate as to suite even persons w͏. cannot eat eggs when cooked in usual way. - *Lois Shafer*

Noodles

2 cups flour
2 eggs - small amount of water
pinch of salt

THEN: Mix together with fork, then knead 'till very thick and dry. Mo͏ flour may have to be added. Roll very thin. Then after rolling thin th͏ were hung on the oven handle or a line by the stove to dry. When alm͏ dry they were taken down, rolled up in a roll and cut to desired siz͏ Shake out the rolled pieces, add a little flour to keep them from stickir͏ together. Put in boiling water and cook. Serve with sauce or add to boil͏ chicken broth for chicken noodles. (My mother would tell us girls v͏ couldn't get married 'till we could roll noodles thin enough to read t͏ paper through them and there could not be wrinkles in the dough. I dor͏ think she wanted us to marry, do you?)

NOW: Today it is much easier. Buy a bag of already made noodles. The͏ are many different kinds today. It is much easier just to buy at our we͏ stocked grocery stores, cook and serve. - *Louise Shafer*

Chicken and Dumplings

Cut up a nice sized young chicken, place in a pot. Fill with water to
over chicken. Season with salt and pepper, and boil until done. Diced
nion and carrots may be added the last half hour of cooking for more
avor and color.

umplings:

1 1/2 cups flour	2 teaspoons baking powder
3/4 teaspoon salt	3 tablespoons shortening
3/4 cup milk	

Blend dry ingredients. Cut in shortening, add milk and mix well. Drop
y spoonful into chicken and meat stock while boiling. Reduce heat and
ook slowly for 10 minutes uncovered, then cover and cook 10 more
inutes. Remove dumplings and meat to platter and thicken broth. Serve.

Fried Chicken

HEN: Kill and dress a chicken, wash it very good in cold water, then
ipe it dry with a linen cloth. Cut up the chicken into pieces, season with
lt and pepper. Sift enough flour to coat each piece.

Put the chicken into a hot frying pan with equal parts of hot bacon
rease and butter, or all butter that has been aged. Cover the frying
hicken and fry slowly, turning often to brown.

When cooked, serve while hot.

OW: Take car - a gallon of gas - car keys and a $20.00 bill. Start car
ith key and drive to the Kentucky Fried Chicken drive up window.
rder chicken and two side dishes as you choose. Get either corn bread or
iscuits with the chicken. Drive to the next window and pay with the
20.00 bill. You'll get two sacks of food. Hurry home and serve while
ot. - *Aileen Warrick*

Chicken Pot Pie

If any chicken is left over after a meal of fried or boiled chicken, then
oil together onion, carrots, potatoes, etc. until tender, add chicken and
roth. Put into a baking dish. Make a pie crust or make biscuits - put on
op, cook in oven till biscuit or crust is done.

Creamed Chicken

Use left over chicken or boil a chicken, bone and cut into bite s
pieces. Set aside.

Heat 1/2 cup butter or fat in skillet, add chopped onion to taste a
cook until tender. Add a scant teacup flour (less if a less thick gravy
desired), blend well. Gradually add 1 quart milk, blend well and cc
until thickened. Add chicken. Serve over toast.

Roast Chicken

Select a young fat chicken, kill and dress. Dry well, salt inside a
out.

Break up dried bread, place in medium bowl. Add salt, thyme a
sage. Cook diced onion in butter until done, but not brown. Add broth
water. Pour over bread, let set until moisture has soaked into bread. Wc
gently to blend onions and seasonings with bread. If dry add a little wat
Gently place bread mixture in chicken. Roast until done.

Pressed Chicken

Clean and cut up your chicken. Stew in just enough water to cov
them. When nearly cooked, season well with salt and pepper. Let the
stew down until the water is nearly all boiled out, and the meat dro
easily from the bones. Remove the bones and gristle; chop the me
rather coarsely, then turn it back into the stew kettle, where the broth w
left (after skimming off all fat), and let it heat through again. Turn it intc
square bread pan, placing a platter on the top, and a heavy weight on t
platter. This, if properly prepared, will turn out like a mold of jelly a
may be sliced in smooth, even slices. The success of this depends up
not having too much water; it will not jelly if too weak, or if the water
allowed to boil away entirely while cooking. A good way to cook c
fowls. - *from the White House Cookbook, year unknown*

Other things - - - -

Egging and Crumbing is dipping molded food into beaten egg, the
rolling in fine crumbs and again dipping in egg. This forms a coati
which hardens immediately when the food is immersed in deep, hot fa
thus aiding in preventing absorption of the cooking fat.

Raising & Butchering Pigs

Many old timers raised pigs, butchered and cured the meat. That was quite an undertaking. After the pig was fed and taken care of for anywhere from six months to a year it was shot in the head, its throat cut and the blood saved in a large vessel and stirred so it would not clot. This was used to make blood sausage. Don't sound good? - it is very tasty when mixed with other ingredients and smoked.

The pig is then scalded; water being heated very hot in a large barrel or anything the animal could be immersed in. Then it was scrapped with sharp scrapers to remove the hair from the hide. It was then gutted. The guts were also saved and cleaned. They were cleaned by turning inside out and the intestine was pulled through two sticks, washed and soaked in salt water and used for casings for sausage later. The animal was cooled, cut up and hams and bacons put in brine to get ready to smoke. Lard was rendered by slowly heating the fat and skin. After the skin became very crisp from this cooking process they are called cracklings. Cracklings are great eating.

What could be kept fresh was roasted, cooked with sauerkraut, boiled or fried. The scrap meat was used to make sausage, headcheese, scrapple, etc. Making sausage was a several day job as meat had to be chopped or ground, seasoned and stuffed into casings, then smoked like ham and bacon. Smoking preserved the meat as well as improved the taste. - *Louise Shafer*

All But the Squeal!

As you can see, every part of the pig was used, nothing went to waste. Thus it was said that "everything was used but the Squeal!*" - *Louise Shafer*

Tip . . .

When baking instructions say "bake in a slow oven", that means 300° to 325°.

Curing Pork in Brine

__THEN:__   To each 400 pounds of meat, make a brine as follows:

> 20 gallons of rain water
> 30 pounds of salt
> 8 ounces of baking soda
> 10 pounds brown sugar
> 1 gallon GOOD molasses

    This fluid should be boiled and skimmed in the morning and left t
cool in a shady place. When cool add five (5) ounces of salt-pete
Dissolve the salt-peter in warm water and stir thoroughly.
    Put meat in barrel and weigh down well and pour brine over it until
is thoroughly covered. It can be left in brine indefinitely, but it is desire
to smoke the meat. It should be taken out of brine in about six weeks to b
smoked.

__NOW:__   I am sure that today most people just buy the meat alread
smoked at the butcher shop. - *Louise Shafer*

Tip . . .

__When baking instructions say "bake in a moderate oven", that mean
350° to 375° and a "hot" oven is 400° or more.__

Scrapple

__THEN:__   Scrapple is made from small scrap pieces of meat and meat tha
is cooked off of the bones of hogs. Cook, either boil or bake, the bone
after all other cuts have been taken off. Remove the meat from the bones
combine with broth. Bring broth and meat to a boil; add salt and any othe
seasonings you may want. Add corn meal, - about 1 cup corn meal to
cups broth - slowly, stirring constantly. Cook about 30 minutes. Pour int
pan and allow to set up. Turn out of pan, cut in thin slices. Fry until wel
browned.

__NOW:__ Not all super markets carry scrapple but some specialty stores dc
Visit your favorite gourmet grocery store and see if they have it available.

To Prepare Pigs' Feet for Pickling

When the pig was scalded the feet were also scalded and scrapped the same as the rest of the pig. Scalding made the hooves come loose and they were removed. The feet were then ready for processing.

Pickled Pigs' Feet

THEN:

4 pig's feet	4 cups vinegar
2 teaspoons whole cloves	1 tablespoon salt
1 bay leaf	1 onion
1/2 teaspoon pepper	

Wash and scrape pig's feet. Boil until meat will slip from bone. Drain. Place meat in bowl. Combine vinegar, and all other ingredients. Boil 30 minutes. Add 2 cups broth in which the pig's feet were cooked. Strain. Pour over pig's feet. Let stand 3 days before using.

NOW: Now days Pickled Pigs' Feet are generally found in a specialty food store or occasionally at a local bar down the road.

Headcheese

1 hog's head
1 hog's tongue
sage and chili powder
salt and pepper

Clean and scrape hog's head. Wash thoroughly. Wash and trim tongue. Cover tongue and head with slightly salted water. Simmer until meat falls from bone. Drain meat. Shred. Season to taste. Mix thoroughly. Pack tightly in bowl. Cover and weight down. Let stand three days. Slice.

Sugar Cure for Ham

1 pint salt
2 tablespoons black pepper
1 teaspoon red pepper
1 teaspoon saltpeter
4 tablespoons brown sugar

Put in skillet and heat real hot, stirring constantly. Rub on meat aft meat has cooled (after butchering).

Put on meat when weather is around 40 and 50. Put in a smoke hou and smoke until cured. One week curing is enough. Or with toda conveniences, wash, dry and apply white smoke liquid once, dry. Cut and put in freezer. Side meat will cure in about 4 days. If you are doi any meat with a bone in it be sure and get the sugar cure worked do into the meat around the bone. - *Wilma Senters, Lawrenceville, Illino from the Myrna (Shafer) Carpita Collection*

Sausage

6 pounds lean fresh pork   3 pounds of chine fat
3 tablespoons salt   2 tablespoons black pepper
4 tablespoons sage   2 tablespoons savory

Chop the pork and fat finely, mix in seasonings. Fill into casing either cleaned intestines of the hog or narrow bags of stout muslin. F these with meat, dip in melted lard and hang them in a cool, dry dark place. **Note:** This sausage is <u>not</u> cooked so keep very cool or frozen.

When ready to cook, take out, if in muslin, make round patties and fry until done. If in cleaned intestines, cut in tied lengths, prick, place in pan with grease, cook slowly, so as not to break casing, until done.

60

To Fry Sausages

Put a small piece of lard or butter into a frying pan. Prick the sausages ith a fork, lay them in the melted grease keep moving them about, rning them frequently to prevent bursting; in ten or twelve minutes they ill be sufficiently browned and cooked. Another sure way to prevent the ses from bursting is to cover them with cold water and let them come to e boiling point; turn off the water and fry them. Sausages are nicely ooked by putting them in a baking pan and browning them in the oven, rning them once or twice. In this way you avoid all smoke and sagreeable odor. A pound will cook brown in ten minutes in a hot oven.

White House Cook Book – date unknown

Blood Sausage

HEN: Butcher two 250 pound pigs, save 1 1/2 gallons of blood. Add 1 '2 cups salt - this will keep blood from clotting.

Prepare tongue, heart, tripe by washing. Boil, save broth. Peel tongue. oil heads, neck and all trimmings until done, remove meat from the ones. Save broth.

Grind all of the meat. Cracklings may also be ground and added to the usage.

Boil 2 gallons broth and 10 pounds of rice until tender. Cool.

Add:

2 ounces allspice	2 ounces poultry seasoning
2 ounces cloves	1 large head of garlic - chopped
4 ounces cinnamon	1 pound pepper

Add ground meat and rice to blood as well as enough broth to make ixture soft enough to stuff into casings. Stuff into casings.

Place sausage in to boiling water and cook until it floats. Cool.

Place sausage in lard to preserve. - *Mary Bolick*

OW: If by chance you would make this sausage now you would robably freeze the sausage rather than immerse it in lard to keep it.

If you just wanted Blood Sausage but did not want to make it then you ould go to the butcher shop or a specialty market and purchase it.

The best parts of the pig that are usually used for roasting are t loin, leg, shoulder, spare rib and pork chops. These cuts were us when fresh. The hams, shoulders and middling (cuts for bacon lesser quality pork) are usually salted, smoked or pickled.

Pork Chops and Fried Apples

Season the pork chops with salt and pepper to taste. Dip in flour a fry in grease until done. Set aside but keep warm.

Slice an apple, cutting them around, about 1/4 inch thick, remove t core, fry in the grease from the pork chops until brown and serve with t pork chops.

Gravy may be made from the drippings and served with the chops a apples.

Roast Pork Loin

Take a good loin roast, score the skin about 3/4 inch apart, place in roaster with a little water, place in a moderate oven. Roast until near do then increase temperature and roast until rind hardens. Serve with ro potatoes, parsnips or carrots and applesauce.

If roast is lean, rub with lard or butter before baking.

Many times when pigs or other animals were butchered the fre meat was shared with numerous families and thus the fresh meat w used up before it could spoil.

The fat on pork should be white and very firm. Lean pork shou have a fine grain. Cook pork thoroughly.

OTHER MEAT RECIPES

Mincemeat

2 pounds meat (beef, venison, elk)
1 pound suet
4 pounds pared apples
4 cups sugar
2 pounds currents
3 pounds raisins
1/2 pound citron (cut fine)
juice & grated rind of 2 oranges
juice and grated rind of 2 lemons
1 pint cider or brandy
1 tablespoon salt
1 1/2 teaspoons nutmeg
1/2 teaspoon mace

Cook slowly the meat in hot water to cover until tender - about 3 hours. Cool and force through food chopper with apples using course blade. Add all remaining ingredients and mix thoroughly. Cook slowly 1 hour. Seal in sterile jars. Makes 12 - 14 pints. Use 1 pint for 8" pie. Bake at 450° for 35 minutes. - *Louise Shafer*

Shepherd's Pie

Cut up enough cold roast beef to make a quart of small, thin slices. Season the meat with salt and pepper and after putting it into a deep earthen dish pour over it a sauce made as follows: Put two tablespoonful of butter into a frying pan, and when it has become hot add two scant tablespoonful of flour. Stir until it is dark brown and then add a pint of water. Season with salt and pepper and boil for three minutes. Pare, boil and mash eight good sized potatoes; then add to them a cupful of boiling milk, a tablespoonful of butter, and salt and pepper to suit the taste. Spread this preparation over meat and sauce, beginning at the side of the dish and working toward the center. Bake for 30 minutes. Other meats beside roast beef may be used in a shepherd's pie if desired.

Toad in the Hole

THEN: This may be made of beef cut into small cubes or of por
sausage. If sausage is used squeeze them out of the skins in balls as larg
as the end of your thumb. Sausage meat will not do. Put either sausage
beef into a deep dish and set them in the oven while you are mixing th
batter. If beef, you will need to put a little water, about a gill, into the dish
Mix a batter with 1/2 pint of milk and the same quantity of flour, (batte
are always made in this manner), one egg well beaten, but no bakin
powder or soda. Put a little salt into the batter and if you are using bee
salt and pepper to taste. Pour the batter directly over the beef.

But with sausages drain off a little of the grease and be careful to mi
the meat evenly through the dish. Bake half an hour in a hot oven. It mu
be eaten as soon as it is cooked.

NOW: Buy some "Bisquick", and hope they have an Impossible Pi
recipe similar to this. - *Lois Shafer*

Savory Pie

Chop together a pound of cold fried steak, some cooked potatoes,
cold boiled onion and moisten with some leftover brown gravy. Put in
deep baking dish, covering the top and sides with a pie crust made of on
breakfast cup of flour and a quarter of a cup of butter, wet to a soft doug
with cold water. Bake and serve hot.

Meat Loaf

1 pound ground beef	1 egg, slightly beaten
2 tablespoons onion chopped	1/4 teaspoon pepper
1 cup milk	1 teaspoon salt
1 cup coarsely broken crackers	2 slices bacon (optional)
or dry bread crumbs	

Combine all ingredients except bacon. Form in loaf. Lay slices of acon across top. Bake in moderate oven for 1 hour. If desired substitute /2 cup uncooked oatmeal for cracker crumbs. Serve with tomato sauce.

Hash

Grind left over roast beef. Add gravy or broth to moisten. Dice otatoes and carrots and chop onion and add to meat. Bake in moderate ven about 45 minutes. Hollow out several places in the meat, break an gg in each hollow and continue to bake until egg is cooked to the desired oneness. Serve hot.

Pasties

Cube a cup each of rutabaga, potato, carrot, and 1/2 cup onion. Cubes hould be about 3/8 inch. Cube 2 or 3 cups of steak-sirloin or any good fat teak- making cubes same size as vegetable cubes. Salt and pepper meat nd vegetable mixture, mix. (Flank steak or a less desirable steak may lso be used but cut at an angle to break up meat fiber and add 2 easpoons of fat).

Make a crust by blending 2 ablespoons lard or whatever you ave and 1 cup finely cut suet vith 3 cups flour. Add 1 easpoon salt and sufficient water o make stiff paste or dough.

Roll out enough dough to nake a crust about 6 by 8 inches. Place 1 cup vegetable/meat mixture on ower side of dough, Dampen edges of dough with water, fold over and eal. Crimp edges to seal well. There should be no holes for the moisture o escape. Bake one hour at 350° or until the crust is golden and pasty is ooked through.

Sewing

The lady of the household did most of her own sewing, maki clothing, bedding and other household items. She sometimes ma clothing for other people and this supplemented the family income. In t very early days all things were stitched by hand. Many women wove th own cloth from material they had made into thread and yarn. Later clc became available to be purchased but still had to be made into shirts, pants, dresses, underclothing, bedding and other household items. All were sewn by hand and if any decorative design was put on them it also was done by hand unless per chance the lady had the availability of lace or ribbon. Some women made their own lace and also embroidered and crocheted designs on the clothing. People generally only had a couple of sets of clothing but with a large family this was a lot to sew for and maintain.

In the about the 1870's sewing machines started to become availab to the housewife. This made sewing go much faster, especially if y consider that one of the very first sewing machines could sew five enti seams while a skilled seamstress could only sew one by hand.

Quilts were another household item that were made from scraps cloth that were available. They were pieced (sewn) together, and a batti and a backing material attached. They were either tied with string or ya or hand quilted.

Another chore was making pillows and bed ticks for the househo These were filled with down and small feathers that were collected wh chickens, ducks and geese were butchered. The small feathers and dov were carefully plucked, cleaned and kept until they could be used at later time.

Tip...

To make cement for repairing china, stoneware or glassware, ad finely powdered quick lime to whites of two eggs to form a thic paste.

MISCELLANEOUS

As there was no corner grocery store, there was not a corner drugstore either. Pioneers had to fend for themselves. They had various remedies and potions to fit their needs, although not nearly the variety that we have today.

Tooth Care

Tooth care has evolved from using a soft stick, chewed and flattened on the end to scrape the teeth, to the variety of tooth brushes we now have.

Various powder concoctions were used from plain salt or soda to brush with, to mixtures made of pulverized chalk and charcoal mixed with spirits of camphor and soap suds. This was mixed into a thick paste and used.

Tooth aches were helped by making a solution of alum and sweet spirits of nitre. One drop would take care of the pain.

Another tooth ache cure was made from alcohol, camphor, opium powder and oil of cloves. Sounds like it would take care of the problem for sure!

Cold Remedy

Colds might be treated with a mixture of lard and turpentine that you would rub on your chest for congestion.

Mustard pack was another method to cure a cold and congestion. It was made of lard and mustard. This was spread on a cloth, placed on the chest and then warm clothes placed over that. (This could also lead to major skin irritation!)

For a bad cough you might have gotten a spoon full of turpentine mixed with sugar.

Onion Cough Syrup

Slice onions, add water and honey. Cook slowly until onions are clear and soft and liquid becomes syrup. Take a spoon full of the syrup to relieve a cough.

Hot Toddy

A hot toddy was the general "cure all" for a cold. Now the tod could be made from various ingredients. One that is very good is lem juice or vinegar, honey, whiskey and hot, hot water. This was given j before bedtime. Like a baby you would sleep. Cure the cold? It certai made you happy and the cold more tolerable.

Healing Salve

2 teaspoons cod liver oil   1/2 teaspoon garlic powder
3 teaspoons glycerin   1 teaspoon honey

Beat well and store in jar.

Hand Lotion

1 cup rose water   1/2 teaspoon honey
1/2 teaspoon glycerin   1/2 teaspoon vinegar

Shake well and store in a bottle.

Tip . . .

Chicken fat, tallow and lanolin from sheep wool also helped keep hands from cracking and becoming sore.

Marigold Lotion

Cut the blossom of a marigold into small pieces. Place in a pan wi lard, cook until blossom shrivels up. Strain and pour into a jar. Use f cuts, bites, and scrapes.

Tip . . .

Solutions made from marigolds were also used as an astringent.

Polish for Ladies Kid Shoes

A fine liquid polish for ladies' kid shoes, satchels, etc., that is easy of application, recommended as containing no ingredients in any manner injurious to leather, is found by digesting in a close vessel at gentle heat, and straining, a solution made as follows: Lampblack one drachm, oil turpentine four drachms, alcohol (trymethyl) twelve ounces; shellac one and one-half ounces, white turpentine five drachms, sandarac two drachms. - *The White House Cook Book, copyright, 1887*

Shoe Repair

Many households had materials and equipment available to repair shoes. When the soles of shoes wore out they were replaced and a lot of pioneers did their own repairs as there was not a cobbler nearby to do the repairs. A cast iron shoe form anvil could be found in many homes with the various sized shoe forms that were interchangeable as needed. They also had awls for punching holes so they could sew the leather and of course tacks if they were needed for the heels of the shoes.

Shoes were "recycled" in that as one child outgrew his or her shoes they were passed down to the next child as they grew into them.

Buckets and Barrels

Did pioneers have metal buckets, tubs or barrels as we know them today? Not likely. Buckets, tubs and barrels were made of wood staves and held together with metal hoops. If water was not kept in these vessels the wood would dry out, shrink and fall apart so they had to be soaked to avoid this problem. Later tin was formed into these items and worked well but would rust if not cared for properly.

Water

Having enough water in the home was a chore to keep up with. As all households water is used and necessary for many purposes.

If your water source was near your home, that was considered convenience. It still had to be brought into the home as needed but it wa nearby and generally plentiful.

Rain water was a source of water and was collected and used in th household. Wooden barrels were set at each valley that was formed b the roof structure of the homes and outbuildings and run-off water wa collected. Early homes did not have gutter systems that we now have o our homes. When the water was low in the barrels there was sediment i the bottom and this had to be cleaned out by dumping and rinsing. Th rain water generally was not used for drinking water. Rain water is "so water" as it does not have any mineral content in it. It was used fc household chores such as clothes washing, cleaning, bathing and washin hair. Hair washed with rain water resulted in the hair being very soft. Rai water, of course, was only available in spring and summer in most area When the barrels were not being used they had wooden lids to keep ou unwanted debris and, in winter, the accumulation of snow and ice tha could cause damage to the barrels.

Some homes, after being established might have a hand dug well if th water table was close enough to the surface, but it took a lot of wor requiring the digging and rocking up of the inside of the well to keep from caving in. This, of course, required the digging of the well, hauling lot of rocks to the site of the well, lowering them into the well an stacking the rocks in a manner that would give good support to the wel walls, making it a solid structure. Then there had to be a way of gettin the water from the bottom of the well. Sometimes it was just a bucke attached to a rope, others might have a winch so the bucket could b winched up and required less work to get the water to the surface.

There were hand pumps but in the very early days they were far an few between. Pumps were a real improvement but still required arn power to raise the water to the surface. The real improvement with th pumps is when they were in the house and there was a sink to pump wate directly in to and the sink drain took the excess water back outside.

If you were real lucky there may be a spring nearby that could b piped into the home and ran back out in a drainage system. It generall ran full time. Metal pipes were generally not available so "piping" wa made with hollowed out logs or logs split in half and hollowed out.

If you were not located near a stream or did not have a well then the water had to be hauled. This generally meant hitching up the horses to a wagon, loading buckets and a barrel or barrels into the wagon and traveling to a water source. There you filled the buckets, lifted them into the wagon and poured them into the barrel. Some barrels had lids but others did not. If a lid was not available then the barrel was generally covered with cloth or maybe an old blanket and tied in place to keep the water from sloshing out on the return trip home.

Hauling water for just the home use was one thing, but if you had to haul water for livestock or to water a garden it was just about a full time job and depending on the distance hauled could take many hours. Any way you want to look at it, you had running water, even if you had to run and get it.

Wash Day

The laundry or wash day was most always the first job on Monday for the lady of the house. Most covered wagons had a wash tub and wash board. The wash tub was used for more than washing clothes. Saturday night bath for the whole family - same water used for all - the last one through the process had pretty dirty water but usually some member of the family would rinse them off with a couple of dippers of clean water. This added some fun if cold water was used.

But, back to the laundry! When people found themselves needing to wash clothing and they did not have a washboard they would use a rock to scrub the clothing on or beat the clothing on. I would imagine this was pretty rough on the clothing, not to say a lot of hard labor for the person doing the washing.

Having a wash board and a tub of some kind was certainly a move up from the rock method. If they were washing in a creek they had wash and rinse water running right by them, although very cold water. If they had moved out of the creek and to wash tubs they had to haul the water and heat it. Some could get their water from the creek, spring or even melting snow. This was hauled, heated, soap added and the clothing scrubbed on the washboard. Of course they had to have rinse water as well, so it too, was hauled but not always heated and just used cold. The white clothing was washed first and then the colored clothing and heavy work clothes. Each piece of clothing was wrung out by hand after t wash and after each rinse.

The wash water was not just thrown out as it could be used for oth cleaning such as scrubbing the wagon inside, if on the trail, the flo steps, porch of your home, if you had one, and cleaning the outhou facility.

Now that the clothes were washed they had to be dried. I imagi while traveling the clothing was hung on the wagons and bushes or fence if handy. After a home was established there generally was a cloth line and this simplified the drying process, except in winter or rainy day Then they were hung in the house to dry or if hung outside and we rained on or frozen, they were still hung in the house to dry! Wi clothing being washed and dried then there was the chore of ironing.

The clothing was dried but now in order to iron you had to sprinkle t clothing to dampen them so they could be ironed properly. Sprinkli clothing was done the day before they were to be ironed. The clothing w laid out and with warm water in a pan you dipped your hand in and th shook the water off of your hand on to the clothing. Now the clothing w wrapped tight in a cloth and this allowed the water to evenly dampen tl clothing. Once the clothing was dampened they had to be ironed in fair short order or they would dry out or worse yet, they would mildew. Tl ladies used "sad" irons or "flat" irons. There were not the irons as v know them today that are heated with electricity and have a device th steams as the iron is used.

When getting ready to iron, the irons were placed on the stove, heate to the proper temperature, generally tested by dampening a finger al touching the iron, and ironing until the iron was too cold and then tl heating and ironing process was repeated until all of the ironing was don While ironing, the clothing was mended if needed and socks darned they had holes in them.

Knowing how the washing was done, the question remains as to whe and how did they get soap? They made it! This also was women's wor This all began with saving ashes and grease of all kinds. Some tallow fats made better soap than others; badger and bear fat being among tl favorites.

Rendering Fat

Any kind of fat that was available was saved. Fat was used for man purposes, one being the making of soap. At butchering tim

rticularly, there was a lot of fat and it was saved and rendered. Now,
ndering fat was time consuming and somewhat dangerous because the
t was very flammable. The fat might be rendered over a camp fire or on
wood stove. Either way, a large kettle was used.

Fat sometimes was rendered by frying the chunks of fat from an
imal. This was particularly dangerous because of the frying grease
ould splatter, burn and in some cases catch fire. It was highly
commended having a lid for the pot to control the splatters and put on
e pot to smother the flames should a fire start.

Another method of rendering the fat was to place water in your kettle
d then add the fat, letting it boil until all of the fat had melted. Than the
ater and fat were set aside, allowed to cool and the fat to harden. Then
e fat was removed from the pan, leaving the water. Any particles of
eat were usually on the bottom of the fat and could be scraped or cut off
d discarded. In both methods the fat needed to be again heated and
rained through a cloth to remove all undesirable debris. Once this was
one the fat was ready for many uses.

Making Lye from Wood Ash

n order to make soap you must have lye. Lye was not available in a
bottle or can as it is today so you made your own. Each time the stove
r campfire pit was cleaned, the ashes were saved. The ashes were placed
a wooden barrel or special wooden ash hopper, covered and kept dry.
hey were saved over a period of time. The barrel or hopper had a hole in
e bottom with a plug. When ready to make lye, water was added to the
sh and left to soak overnight. When it was time to gather the lye, the plug
as removed and more water added so the liquid would start to drip from
e hole. This liquid is lye and needs to be caught in a glazed crock or in a
lass container. Do not let the lye touch your skin as it can result in a
urn.

Lye must be of certain strength in order to make soap. To test the
trength of the lye an egg or potato is placed in it. If the egg or potato
oats just below halfway, the lye water is the right strength. If it is
ubmerged too much, the water must be boiled until the egg or potato
oat at the proper level. If the egg or potato pops up too much, then more
ater must be added in order to dilute the lye water. When all is correct,
e lye water may be used for making soap.

73

Soap Making

4 1/2 pound clean fat. Strain before using. Empty 1 can of lye i
cold water; add 1/2 cup Borax and 1/2 cup ammonia. When this is c
slowly pour into grease which is warm but not hot. Stir 10 minutes or u
it is like a heavy cream. When hard enough cut into squares. - *Caro*
Adams

Tip . . .

**When using lye water, measure to the amount of water called for
the soap recipe. Add more to your mixture if the fat does not dissol
properly.**

Hard Soap
(Without boiling)

Melt 5 1/2 pounds of clean grease - tallow or lard - in a pan over
fire until dissolved. Set aside to cool. Empty 2 1/2 pints of prepared wo
ash lye or the contents of 1 can of lye into 2 1/2 pints of cold water. Wh
the grease has become cold or about 120 degrees now slowly po
dissolved lye into the grease, stir until it mixes thoroughly and also m
with this 1/3 box of 20 Mule Team Borax. Let stand until it begins to
thick and then pour into mold -- a wooden box will do. Cover with an
blanket, carpet, gunny sack, etc. and cut into squares. *Note: This so*
was used primarily for the weekly clothes washing. - Aunt Net *[Net*
(Hand) Garrison] - From the Susan Hand Collection - ***Reprint w***
permission, copyrighted - 1992 MAGGIE, by Myrna (Shafer) Carpita

Toilet Soap

2 pounds beef tallow	2 pounds salsoda
1 pound salt	1 ounce oil of camphor
1 ounce oil of bergamot	1 ounce borax

Boil slowly for one hour. Stir often. Remove from heat, let stand un
cool. Heat again slowly until liquid enough to pour into molds. Dip
cold water.

Making Candles

Ever hear the term "went to bed with the chickens"? Well, when it gets dark chickens will go into their coop and roost. Now, in the early pioneer days the only light available in the evenings was from the campfire or fireplace. That was just not very good light. If there was not any light, then after dark there was not much to do but go to bed, thus "went to bed with the chickens".

The pioneers did have what was called a grease lamp. They would fill a small bowl with fat and put a twist of cloth in the fat, allowing it to soak up the fat and leaving just the end stuck over the edge of the bowl. The fat would wick up to the end of the cloth and could be lit for a "little" light. This did not give off much light and smoked a lot and probably did not smell very good either. In fact, the pioneers learned to put various herbs in the fat so it would smell better.

The next best thing that came along and gave off better light were candles made from fat. To do this, cords (sometimes twists of grass) were tied on to a stick and let hang down. Fat was melted in a pot and the cords were dipped down into the fat and slowly pulled up, coating the cord with a layer of fat. This was repeated numerous times until a candle of a desired diameter was formed. There were also candle molds available and this made candle making go a little faster.

The main drawback, again, was smoke and smell and if these candles were not kept in a cool place when stored they would melt and droop into a glob. Candles were another reason that all fats or tallow were saved.

The very best thing for candle making was bees wax. It burned clean and gave off good light and did not smell bad.

There were various types of candlestick holders and lanterns made to put the candles in.

Later candles were replaced with coal oil lamps. These lamps had a reservoir filled with oil and a wick down into it. The oil wicked up and could be lit. These wicks were fairly wide so gave off a better light than the candle. The wicks had to be trimmed

75

and they smoked, and if you had a chimney on the light they became dir
and had to be cleaned. Apparently if you soaked the wick in vinegar an
dried them they did not smoke as much.

The advantage of chimneys on a lamp is you did not have to hold yo
hand in front of the flame when you moved the lamp. Also some lam;
were available with a wire handle and chimney so you could take
outside and it could be hung up. - *Myrna (Shafer) Carpita*

<h2 style="text-align:center">Tip . . .</h2>

**Mineral deposits in your tea kettle can be
removed by emptying all water and
refilling kettle with vinegar. Let set until
mineralization has dissolved. Or leave a
little water in the kettle, adding some
small, clean pebbles and swishing around
until mineral deposits have disappeared.**

<h2 style="text-align:center">Tip . . .</h2>

**Baking Powder will remove tea or coffee stains from china pots o
cups.** - *Charlotte Kistler*

<h2 style="text-align:center">Tip . . .</h2>

**Need to clean a knife – rub the knife blade with brick dust. Use
damp cloth dipped in brick dust, rub well until clean, rinse and dry
This will remove any rust and will shine the blade.**

To Remove Linen Stains

Rub the stains with soft soap, apply a starch paste, dry in the sun an
wash out in cold water. Repeat several times is necessary.

Herbs and Spices

If a person knows what to look for there are various plants that grow in the wild that will lend themselves to adding flavor to various foods. The pioneers knew some of them and relied on them in the early days but also brought their own seeds for other herbs.

Wild Garlic - grows wild in Montana. It is very good but has a mild flavor in comparison to the tame garlic. It is also small so requires a lot of searching. Garlic is used in meats, vegetables, salads, dressings and sauces.

Wild Onion - grows wild in Montana. It is very good but also has a mild flavor. Again, it is small and also requires a lot of searching. Onions are used in stews, salads, meats, and with various vegetables.

It might be noted here that the milk cows, in the early spring, have very little problem finding the garlic and onion. They also like it and it is very evident they are sampling these morsels as the flavor can be very strong in their milk.

Mint - The mint plant grows wild also in Montana along streams and in other damp places. Adds good flavor. There are several kinds and they each have their own distinct flavor. Mint, added to peas gives extra flavor. Also add mint to beverages and fruits for an extra sparkle.

The pioneers probably brought seeds and starts of the following:

Chives - They have a mild flavor early in the spring but get stronger later in the summer. Chives can be dried but lose their flavor when kept a long period. Great in cottage and cream cheeses, scrambled eggs, soups. Wonderful on toasted, buttered bread.

Dill - Dill was planted and kept in the home garden for the purpose of canning. Add to sour cream sauces, coleslaw or potato salad. It dries well.

Caraway - This grows well here and produces an abundance of seed to be stored for winter use. Add to cream-puff batter and fill with creamed ham. Good in salads such as coleslaw.

Horseradish - Roots and seed were brought along and planted. The roots are used to make a horseradish sauce. Adds zest to meats, fish, cheese and eggs.

Basil, Rosemary, Sage, and Thyme - These herbs grow well here and were kept in the herb garden and dried for later use. These can be used alone or in combination with one another.

Basil is good in vegetables, soufflés and meat.

Rosemary is distinctively fresh and sweet, but potent. Good with meat, dumplings, biscuits. Its flavor is complementary with garlic powder and parsley.

Sage - (not sage brush) - can be use as whole leaf or ground. Great stuffing for poultry or pork. Good in soups.

Thyme - Blends well with other herbs. Good in soups and chowders and with vegetables.

Parsley - Grows well in Montana. Has a light flavor and is used as an accent color in many foods.

Other spices and herbs were brought along or later were available the various stores.

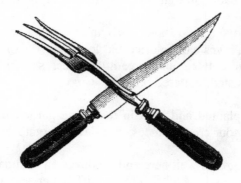

PRESERVES

Preserving food is an art in itself. If produce is not selected and prepared properly there can be a multitude of problems. Produce must be fresh and ripe, but not overripe to have the best results.

Home canned and dried foods will keep for a long period of time. This what the pioneers needed due to no corner store, shortness of seasons and lack of transportation to import fresh fruits and vegetables as we have now. Early, before jars were available, crocks were used for storage of reserves and, large quantities, such as pickles, were stored in barrels.

Piccalilli

Chop up one peck of green tomatoes with 8 large onions. Mix thoroughly with 1 cup salt and let stand overnight. Next morning drain thoroughly and add 1 quart vinegar and 1/2 gallon water. Boil 20 minutes in enamel kettle. Drain through a sieve. Put the mixture back in kettle and add 1 1/2 quarts vinegar, 2 pounds sugar, 1/2 pound mustard seed, 2 teaspoons each ground black pepper and ground cinnamon, 1 level tablespoon ground ginger, whole cloves and whole allspice, 1/2 teaspoon cayenne pepper. Boil 15 minutes, stirring frequently. Put into glass jars and seal.

Sweet Ripe Tomato Pickles

Pare and weigh ripe tomatoes and put in jar, cover with vinegar, stand three days, pour off vinegar, add 5 pounds brown sugar to every 7 pounds tomatoes, spice to taste, cook slowly on back of stove all day. Use cinnamon, mace and a little clove. Put in jars hot, seal. - *Lawrence County Extension, Lawrenceville, Illinois*

Pickled Green Tomatoes

One peck of green tomatoes, six sliced large onions; six red peppers chopped; mix these and throw over them 1 cup salt; let them stand overnight; in the morning drain off. Layer in cooking pot the tomatoes, onions, red peppers, 1 cup sugar, 1 tablespoon ground allspice, 1 tablespoon cinnamon, 1 teaspoon cloves, 1 tablespoon mustard. Cook 15 minutes in 2 quarts water and 1 quart vinegar. Put in jars hot, seal.

Bread and Butter Pickles

Slice:

    10 big cucumbers or 12-15 medium
    4 medium onions

Soak in 3/4 cup salt in 1 gallon water. Let stand 3 hours; drain.

Mix:

    4 cups sugar
    1 quart vinegar
    2 cups water
    2 tablespoons each celery seed and mustard
    seed
    1 1/2 teaspoons turmeric

Simmer for 5 minutes.

Add cucumbers and onions. Cook until clear (10 or 15 minutes). not boil or they will become leathery. Fill jars; seal.

A pinch of alum in each jar will make pickles crisper. - *Myr (Shafer) Carpita*

Watermelon Pickles

Peel and trim the pink part from the rind of one watermelon (disca green part of rind) and soak overnight in water that has been sligh salted. Drain. Put pink rind in fresh water and boil until tender. To 1 p vinegar add 2 pounds sugar. In a bag place 4 ounces stick cinnamon, ounces whole cloves. Boil vinegar, sugar and spices for about 5 minut Pour over rind and let stand 24 hours. Repeat this procedure the next t days and on the last day heat all ingredients together, boiling a fe minutes. Place in jars and seal.

Carrot Pickles

Cut small carrots into slices an inch thick and steam until tend Place in jar and cover with hot vinegar, sweetened and spiced to tas Seal.

Pickled Horseradish

Dig horseradish roots, wash well and grate fine.

1 cup finely ground horseradish root
1 1/2 teaspoons brown sugar
3 tablespoons vinegar
1/2 teaspoon salt

Combine all ingredients. Let stand overnight before using. It will be very, very hot for several days - use sparingly. Makes 3/4 cup. - *Louise Shafer*

Tip . . .

Various fruits such as peaches, plums and pears were also pickled and put aside for use later on.

Oiled Pickles

small pickles – 100
1 teaspoon black pepper
1 quart small onions
2 ounces celery seed

1/4 pound ground mustard
1/4 pound whole mustard
1 pint olive oil
2 quarts vinegar

Wash and with a cloth rub the cucumbers well; peel the onions and slice both in thin slices. Put a layer of cucumbers and one of onions, then a good sprinkling of salt, then repeat the layers and salt, continuing until all is used. On top place a weight and stand over night. In the morning, drain. Put a tablespoonful of powdered alum in sufficient cold vinegar to cover the pickles and let them stand until afternoon. Drain again. Do not waste this vinegar as it can be used for other pickles. Put the cucumbers and onions into jars, mix all the remaining ingredients together, gradually adding the oil and vinegar and pour over them. Seal. - *The Peoples Home Recipe Book by Mrs. Alice G. Kirk, 1913*

Buffalo Berry Catsup

Cover berries with water and boil 5 to 6 hours, and then rub throug sieve. To every 3 quarts of juice add 2 quarts sugar, 1 teaspoon cinnamo 2/3 teaspoon cloves, 2/3 teaspoon allspice, 1/2 teaspoon mustard, 1, teaspoon red pepper or pinch; 1 teaspoon salt; 1/2 cup vinegar; boil until thickens.

Tomato Catsup

One basket tomatoes, 1 pint vinegar, 1 cup sugar, 2 tablespoons eac cinnamon, allspice, cloves, 1 tablespoon red pepper, 1/2 cup salt, 3 or onions. Cut tomatoes into small pieces and cook until thin and juic Strain through sieve, working as much pulp through as possible. Put o stove and add ingredients, chopping fine and tying spices in a cloth. Bo until the right consistency and bottle hot.

Tip . . .

Extra tomatoes? Slice them and dry them. Keep in a tightly seale dry environment. When you need tomatoes in soup or stew throw in handful. Cook until reconstituted.

Cucumber Catsup

Large ripe cucumbers. Remove seeds, grate. Measure pulp. For 1 pir pulp, add 1/2 pint vinegar, 1/4 teaspoon cayenne pepper, 1 teaspoon salt, large tablespoons grated horseradish. Allow cucumber pulp to drain we then add ingredients, mix thoroughly, bottle and seal. This does nc require cooking. (Refrigerate this or eat within a short period of time).

Jams, Jellies, Preserves, etc.

What Are They?

Jelly has great clarity, being made from juice only.
Jams, butters and pastes are purees of increasing density.
Preserves, marmalades and conserves are bits of fruit cooked to a translucent state in heavy syrup.

Pectin

Pectin content is essential in jelly and jam to make the fruit and juices thicken. Pectin, when combined with sugar or other sweeteners - except artificial ones - is found naturally in most fruits, being the highest in apples. The natural pectin in fruit can be activated only by cooking - but cooking quickly, both in heating the fruit to help  start the juice and later when juice or pulp is boiled together with sugar. Too slow cooking or boiling too long can reduce the gelling property of pectin. Other fruits that are high in natural pectin are red currants, gooseberries, plums and cranberries.

Before commercial pectin was available, apple juice was added to less pectin rich juices to make them gel. This combination still works. Apple pectin can be made at home to add to the non-jelling juices of raspberries, pears, chokecherries, elderberries, peaches, cherries, strawberries, pineapple or rhubarb.

To make pectin from apples, remove stems and buds, cut apples in quarters without peeling or coring. Place apples in a kettle, cover with cold water - just barely to the top of the apples - cover and cook slowly for 30 minutes or until fruit is quite soft. Place apples in a cloth to strain. Allow to strain fully without squeezing. You will have about 3 quarts of juice. Boil this juice down to about a 1/6 or 1/8 of its original volume. This will give you 1 1/2 to 2 cups of heavy, almost ropy syrup.

Use immediately or to store the pectin for later use, strain and pour the hot pectin into 1/2 pint canning jars. Seal. Store in cool, dry, dark place.

To use the homemade pectin add 1/2 to 3/4 cup apple pectin to 4 cups, low-pectin fruit juice in a large kettle and bring to a boil. Add 2 to 3 cups sugar for the amount of fruit juice used and boil rapidly until t jelly stage is reached. Skim, ladle into hot glasses, seal.

There are various tests for the pectin content in fruit but the simples is to use materials that are readily available in most homes.

Stir together 1 teaspoon of cooked fruit juice and 1 tablespoon rubbing alcohol - everyday 70 percent kind. If this mixture forms one b clot that can be picked up with a fork you will not need to use ex pectin. If it makes only small clots that do not clump together you w have to add pectin. DO NOT EVER TASTE THE SAMPLES of this te as rubbing alcohol is poison!

Current Jelly

Boil 4 quarts of currants in 1 quart of water for about 1/2 hour. Strain through cloth. Bring juice to boil, add 1 cup sugar per cup of juice. Continue to boil at rolling boil. Boil about 20 minutes or until jelly sheets from spoon. Skim and pour into jars. Seal

Gooseberry Jelly

Pick ripe gooseberries, wash, and remove stems and blossom end Place in pan with equal amount of water bring to boil. Boil about 2 minutes. While hot, strain through a cloth.

Measure juice, add equal amount of sugar. Stir until mixed well. Bo about 20 minutes or until jelly sheets on spoon. Remove from heat, skir and pour hot into jars, seal.

Mint Jelly

Collect fresh mint leaves. Measure mint leaves by packing in a 1 cu measure. Pour 1 cup boiling water over the mint leaves. Let stand for hour. Press juice from leaves. To each cup of apple juice, add tablespoons of mint extract and bring to a boil. Add sugar, about 3/4 cu sugar per cup of juice. Boil about 20 minutes or until jelly sheets c spoon. Remove from heat, skim, and pour hot into jars, seal.

Apple Jelly

Wash about 3 pounds of apples (crab apples are excellent for jelly). emove stems and blossom ends. Quarter; place in pan and add enough ater to just come to top of apples. Cover, bring to boil, reduce heat and mmer for 20 to 25 minutes or until apples are soft. Place cooked apples a strainer lined with cloth to extract juice.

Measure 4 cups apple juices into a kettle, add 2 tablespoons lemon ice, if desired, and add 4 cups sugar, stir well. Bring to a rolling boil and oil until mixture sheets from a spoon. Remove from heat, skim, and pour nmediately into jars and seal.

Tip . . .

Wild Black Currants or Bear Currants make good jelly to go with leat. These are found along creeks in the mountains. They do not row naturally in the valleys. Use Current Jelly receipt to make this.

Apple Butter

After the juice for the apple jelly has been xtracted take the remaining pulp and put through a eve. Measure pulp and add sugar, a cup of sugar each cup of pulp. Add cinnamon and cloves to uit your taste. Boil about 20 minutes, stirring as to not allow sauce to tick. Pour, hot into jars, seal.

Gooseberry Conserve

1 1/2 quarts gooseberries stem and blossom ends removed
1 medium orange (unpeeled, chopped)
4 cups sugar
1 cup seedless raisins

Combine all ingredients. Heat slowly to boiling, stirring until sugar issolves. Cook almost to jellying point - about 30 minutes. As mixture nickens, stir frequently to prevent sticking. Pour into jars, seal.

Apple Chokecherry Jelly

Use equal parts apple and chokecherry juice. Place in kettle, bring boil, add sugar – 1 cup sugar to 1 cup juice. Boil until jelly sheets fr spoon. Skim and pour into jars. Seal

Elderberry Jam

Pick and clean 2 quarts elderberries. Add 6 cups sugar and 1/4 c vinegar. Bring slowly to boiling, stirring occasionally until sugar dissolved. Cook rapidly until thick. Stir mixture so it does not stick. Po hot, into jars, seal.

Strawberry Preserves

Combine 3 quarts ripe strawberries, 9 cups sugar, 1/4 cup lemon juice and 1/4 teaspoon salt. Let stand 3 or 4 hours. Cook over low heat, stir until sugar is dissolved. Boil rapidly until berries seem almost transparent. Skim, ladle into jars, seal.

Fruit Syrup

Prepare juice from any fruit that you might have. Boil juice until reduces by half. Stir in a lump of butter and cool. If juice is tart you mig add sugar to taste.

Mock Maple Syrup

Place 2 cups white sugar in pan. Brown the sugar until dissolved. Ad water, stirring constantly until it reaches a syrup consistency. Add a pie of butter and maple flavoring. Serve warm with pancakes or waffles.
Pauline Hartwig from the Louise Shafer Collection

Chokecherry Syrup
Excellent on pancakes!

Pick ripe chokecherries. Wash and put in kettle, add water to top of berries - boil until the skin on the berries has popped. Remove from heat, strain through a cloth.

Measure juice and sugar amounts cup for cup. Place in pan and bring to a rolling boil. Boil 20 minutes. Pour immediately into jars and seal.

Tip . . .

If honey is substituted for sugar there will be a distinct flavor change.

Tip . . .

Jellies or jams made with honey must be cooked longer than those based on sugar.

How to Preserve a Husband

B e careful in your selection. Do not choose too young, and take such as has been reared in good moral atmosphere. Some insist on keeping them in a pickle, while others keep them in hot water. This only makes them sour and sometimes bitter. Even poor varieties may be made sweet, tender and good by garnishing them with patience, well-sweetened with smiles and flavored with kisses to taste. Then wrap them in a mantle of charity, keep warm with a steady fire of domestic devotion and serve with peaches and cream. When thus prepared, they will keep for years. (One who knows.) – *from Mrs. R.E. Ewing, Hurricane Homemaker's Club, York, N.D., Recipes From Many Lands, N.D. Homemaker's Club - date unknown*

Honey

Honey may be used in preparing many foods and old timers utilize this natural commodity. Along the creeks and river bottoms where there were large stands of cottonwood trees, there were also wild honey bees making the old hollow trees their hives. They stored the honey they collected from the flowers all summer in these trees.

The trick was how to harvest the honey without getting stung as the bees were very protective of their hoard. This was their winter food store. After the openings the bees were using were located, rags or some other

 material that would smoke rather than burn up when set on fire, was attached to a long stick and the bees were "smoked". It did not kill them, just sort of made them more manageable. The brave soul who took it upon himself to rob the tree also took extra care to wear long sleeves, gloves and pant legs tied tightly around his ankles. The face was covered with cheese cloth. The tree was either opened up by removing a piece of it and the honey removed

being careful to leave some for the bees so they would survive and supply another crop, or the tree was chopped or sawed down and the honey removed. Often the honey stealers would try to take a portion of the tree that they thought housed the queen. They could take it home and have hive for their own use. If they got the queen, the bees would follow them home. This was how tame honey bees got started.

Now they had the honey, what next? The bee's store the honey in combs made of wax (beeswax). To separate the two it needs to be heated (today there is a spinning process to do this). The honey comb can either be set in the sun and the clear honey will drip out or heated in the oven. This is pure honey. There is also what is called bee bread and this is what is fed to the young bees. This is also extracted the same way but then needs to be strained to take out the dark material in it. This honey is darker and has quite a different taste but is still good. After separation the honey can be stored in jars, crocks, etc., in a cool, dry place and will keep indefinitely. Pure honey will crystallized, which does not harm it. To liquefy after it has hardened or crystallized, just set the container of honey in a pan of warm water and keep it warm until it is liquid again. - *Louis Shafer*

VEGETABLES

Dried Vegetables & Fruits

Dried vegetables, such as beans, lentils and grains were the primary vegetable source for the pioneers as there were very few storage problems with them. They did, however, have to have the moisture restored to them by soaking overnight, in most cases, before cooking. They could be prepared without soaking, if they are covered with cold water and cooked slowly.

Dried fruits were well treasured by the pioneer. Apples were easily dried and kept well. They were peeled (sometimes not), cored, cut into thin slices and placed in the sun to dry. They could be eaten by the slice or soaked in water and made into a wonderful apple pie in the dead of winter. Other fruits and berries were also dried as were some made into fruit leather and stored for future meals.

The Root Cellar

Fresh salads and vegetables, particularly in the winter months, were not the same as we know them now. Although summer months produced a bounty of greens from the wild and vegetables from gardens, winter months did not have the same variety.

The root cellar allowed the pioneer to keep many foods that would otherwise spoil. The cellar, when properly built, would keep a constant cool temperature and kept foods from freezing in the winter and kept them cool in the summer. The problems encountered with the root cellar were burrowing animals and after heavy rains or snow run off it might become flooded and muddy.

Cabbage was one vegetable that would keep for a few months after harvest if it was pulled and hung upside down in a protected area such as the root cellar. Root crops such as carrots, onions, potatoes, parsnips, beets, rutabagas and turnips kept well. They might be used in salads as well as being prepared in other ways. Various types of squash and apples kept well in the root cellar also.

89

Tip . . .

Anything that grows underground, start the cooking process in co water.

Anything that grows above the ground, start off in boiling water.
- *Charlotte Kistler*

Cabbage Salad

THEN: Put one pint vinegar in a pan and let boil. Beat the yolks of eggs, add 2 heaping teaspoonful of sugar, a pinch of salt and a spoonful mustard, also a lump of butter the size of an egg: stir into the boilin vinegar and beat until cool. Pour over thinly sliced cabbage. Serve.

NOW: Go to the Deli section of the grocery store and ask the clerk f cabbage salad. Comes in 1/2 pints, pints, or as you choose. Go to t check out and pay for the cabbage salad. Take home and serve. - *Aile Warrick*

Cold Slaw

THEN: Chop with one small head of cabbage two hard boiled eggs. Ta one-half cup of sour cream, one tablespoon of sugar, a little salt a pepper, and a teaspoon of celery seed. Beat all together, then add o teacup of vinegar and pour over cabbage. If this is put in a tight vessel will keep several days.

NOW: Go to the store; buy a package of slaw mix. Put in bowl and m up the dressing mix that comes in the packet. - *Lois Shafer*

Slaw

Slice cabbage very thin. Add mayonnaise, a little vinegar, and sug to taste. Add a little milk to a cream consistency. Serve chilled.

Tip . . .

Another way to keep cabbages is to cut them off near the head an carry to cellar with leaves on, break off the leaves and pack th cabbages in a light box with stems upward. When the box is near full cover with loose leaves and put the lid on to keep rats out. The should be kept in a dry cellar. - *The Peoples Home Recipe Book I Mrs. Alice G. Kirk, 1913*

90

Sauerkraut

Select firm, mature heads of cabbage. Shred or slice on a kraut slicer. lace a 1 to 2 inch layer of shredded cabbage in a crock. Sprinkle with lt, repeat process until crock is filled - about 20 pounds of cabbage to '2 pound salt. Place a glass pie pan, or plate on top of cabbage, weigh wn with something heavy so cabbage will stay in brine. Allow kraut to rment, skimming each day. Allow to process 2 to 4 weeks depending pon temperature. Put in jars and seal.

Ruth Shafer's Sauerkraut Salad

2 cups of sauerkraut
1 cup celery
1/2 cup of green pepper
1/4 cup of chopped onion
1 can (4 ounces) pimientos (chopped not too thin)

Put cold water over kraut and rinse well. Put all of the vegetables in owl.

Bring to boil 1/2 cup of sugar, 1/2 teaspoon salt and 1/4 cup of inegar. Pour over the vegetables and mix well (hot). Mix well and chill vernight. - *Aileen Warrick*

Tomatoes

Often times, due to a very short growing season in Montana, tomatoes o not ripen on the vine. What to do with all those green tomatoes?? reen tomato preserves can be made or green fried tomatoes may be repared.

Of course, green tomatoes may be rapped in paper, placed in a box and put a dark, cool place. Over a short period f time the tomatoes will ripen and are ery good sliced and served or canned into tewed tomatoes, tomato paste, catsup or auce.

Green Fried Tomatoes

3 large green tomatoes	pinch of salt
1/3 cup flour	2 eggs
1/2 cup cornmeal	3/4 teaspoon salt
1/8 teaspoon black pepper	1/3 cup oil
2 tablespoons hard cheese	
(Parmesan for example)	

Core and slice tomatoes 1/2 inch thick. Season with salt. Beat egg Place flour in dish. Mix remaining ingredients. Dip tomato slices in flo dip in egg; coat with cornmeal mixture. Heat oil in skillet. Cook tomato slices 3 to 4 minutes or until golden brown, turn and cook other side golden brown. Serve warm.

Turnips

Cut in small bits; boil one half hour or until tender with a pinch soda in the water. Drain, add teaspoon each salt and sugar. A lump butter and a little cream, chop with spoon and serve hot.

Buttered Beets

Wash the beets and place in a pan and cover with water. Cook un they start to get tender. Remove from the hot water and cool. While st warm the outer skin may be removed by softly squeezing the bee Remove the outer layer of skin, slice beets and return to the pan with little water. Continue to cook until well done, drain water and add butte Serve hot.

Tip . . .

In the summer the greens from the beets can be cooked until lim and a little vinegar and oil added for a tasty summer side dish.

Beet Salad

Boil some beets, slice and let stand in vinegar overnight. Mix one large cup of chopped beets; one large cup of chopped cabbage; one small onion, about the size of a silver dollar, chopped very fine and a little salt. For the dressing take 4 tablespoonful of butter, 1 tablespoonful of flour, 1 tablespoonful of sugar, 1 teaspoonful of salt, 1 teaspoonful of dry mustard, 1 cup of vinegar, 1 cup of milk, 3 eggs and a speck of cayenne pepper. Let the butter get hot, add the flour and stir until smooth, being careful not to brown, add milk stir and boil up. Place the saucepan in another pan containing hot water. Beat eggs; salt and mustard; add vinegar and stir into boiling mixture. Continue stirring until it thickens. - Mrs. J. R. Morton, *1913 Tested Recipes, by the Ladies Aid Society, 1st Baptist Church, Dillon, Montana*

Cucumber Salad

Slice cucumbers, place in bowl, and sprinkle with salt to taste and add a small amount of vinegar. Let set at room temperature a few hours before serving.

In various areas of the United States different wild plants had a variety of uses in the everyday diet. In the Bannack area the summer season was quite short and therefore not the variety of plants that might be found in the Midwest or South. Still, the old timers managed to have a variety of foods in their diets. The Indians taught the "white man" about various edible plants also, such as the Bitterroot.

Wilted Greens

Pick the "greens" - dandelion, mustard, beets, pigweed, etc. - remove all stems and brown leaves. Wash in several waters, drain. Place in pan - do not add water. Cover and cook slowly until thoroughly wilted. Serve with butter, salt and pepper. Also this is good with a little vinegar added.

Dandelion greens are excellent in salads and as cooked greens, but be sure and pick them when plants are young as old plants are bitter!

Wilted Lettuce Salad

Take leaf lettuce, chop green onion, fry baco crisp, add vinegar, and sugar, mix and pour hot ove lettuce. Dandelion greens were also used for th salad or as part of the greens. - *Louise Shafer*

Cattail spikes were harvested in early spring and prepared as food. Also the roots of the cattail were used for food.

Leaves and stalks from the cattail were used for weaving chai seats and basketry.

The soft down from the mature cattail spikes were often used fo upholstery stuffing.

Oyster Plant (Salsify)

Wash oyster plant root, scrape carefully. Slice or leave whole a desired. Cover with water. Boil until tender. Brown in hot cooking fa season with salt and pepper. If desired, dip the boiled oyster plant i slightly beaten diluted egg. Roll in bread crumbs. Brown in hot fat.

Tip . . .

Watercress - watercress was picked and used for salads. Care must b taken in identifying watercress and not confuse it with other "not s good for you" plants.

More Greens

Early in the spring the new tender shoots were gathered from
Greasewood and prepared. They were steamed or boiled and served like
other greens.

Pig weed was another green that was gathered early in the spring and
used in salads and cooked greens.

Asparagus was another vegetable that was cultivated and later could
be found in and near cemeteries. The mature greenery of the asparagus
was used in floral arrangements for the graves. The seeds spread, thus in
early spring there was an abundance of asparagus near the old cemeteries
and can still be found at the cemeteries and along the roadways.

Tip . . .

Dry mustard is made by grinding mustard seed to a fine powder. The
flavor is determined by the type of mustard seed used. The black or
dark brown mustard seed has a stronger, more pungent flavor than
the larger white, or beige colored mustard seed. The mustard seed is a
small round seed and the whole seed is also used in pickling and
canning.

Mustard

Put 2 large teaspoons of dry mustard into a bowl and pour warm
water over to make a stiff paste, rub smooth, add 1/2 cup of vinegar, one
tablespoon of sugar and a pinch of salt, and the beaten yolks of 2 eggs);
stir the mixture until it thickens, then add a piece of butter the size of an
egg.

Vinegar

Vinegar can be made from sweet cider that is allowed to sour.
Also wine may be exposed to air for a few days and it will turn to
vinegar.

Mayonnaise

To the yolks of 2 eggs add by degrees (add first only a drop or two a time) 1/2 pint of olive oil, taking care to blend each portion with the e before adding more (this should be as smooth as honey). Dilute wi lemon juice or vinegar to the consistency of thick cream. Season with sa a little cayenne pepper, and half teaspoonful of mustard. Ke refrigerated.

French Dressing

1/2 cup salad oil
4 tablespoons vinegar or lemon juice
1/4 teaspoon paprika
1/4 teaspoon salt
2 teaspoons sugar
cayenne to taste

Combine dry ingredients and vinegar. Add oil slowly, beati constantly, until thick. Honey may be substituted for sugar.

Dishwashing

Dishwashing was a chore after every meal or after any cooki project. Pioneers generally had a dish pan. Now in talking about dish pan, this probably was not just used for washing dishes. It could be used for washing small batches of clothing, giving the baby a bath or even making bread.

Dishwashing required the hauling and heating of water. Soap was added to the dish washing water and then another pan with rinse water or just heated water poured over the washed dishes to rinse them. Then they were dried and put away until the next meal.

Potatoes

Potatoes were a winter staple in the root cellar as they kept well and were a welcome addition to meals. They were baked, steamed, fried or smashed but no matter how they were prepared they were nutritious and filling.

Potato Soup

Peal four good sized potatoes and cut into small cubes, add one medium size onion, chopped to 2 tablespoons butter. Sauté until nearly done. Add two cups water, salt to taste and boil until potatoes are well done and water has nearly cooked off. Stir to keep from sticking. Add 2 1/2 cups whole milk and heat. Serve hot with crackers or toast. Note: cheese may be added and a tablespoon of flour added to thicken the soup.

Corn Chowder

THEN: In the spring plant and water the corn till it has matured in the fall of the year. Then harvest the corn ears - cut corn from the cob. Then cook the corn till kernels are tender. Mash kernels and then add a pint of milk, salt and pepper to taste and simmer till corn tastes where you like it. (Use about 4 ears of cut off corn kernels).

NOW:

    2 15 1/2 ounces cans cream corn
    6 slices bacon fried crisp and broken into pieces
    1/2 cup chopped celery
    1/2 cup onion
    2 cups milk

Combine all ingredients and simmer 30 minutes. Before serving you can garnish with grated, shredded cheese.

The real short way today is to go to the store, buy a can of corn chowder soup and prepare as directed on can. - *Betty Hanson*

Corn on the Cob

Pick corn fresh from the garden. Husk and clean well. Place water
the stove to boil. Add a little salt, sugar and corn. Boil about five minu
until done. Serve with butter, salt and pepper.

Escalloped Corn

6 ears of cooked corn or 1 can of corn or 1/2 cup dried corn*

1/2 cup corn liquid	3 tablespoons cream
1 teaspoon sugar	1/8 teaspoon pepper
1 teaspoon salt	2 tablespoons flour
1 cup bread crumbs	1 tablespoon butter

Cut fresh boiled corn, too old to serve on cobs, from the cob' or use t
pulp of one can of corn.

Mix corn with salt, pepper, flour and sugar and add the liquids. M
the butter, mix with the bread crumbs and cover bottom of a pudding di
with half of the crumbs, add the corn mixture and cover the rest with t
crumbs. Bake in a moderate oven about 20 minutes and serve hot.

*If using dried corn, soak overnight and then cook until soft. Use
directed as with other corn.

Corn-Meal Mush

1/2 cup corn meal
2 3/4 cups water
1/2 teaspoon salt

Sprinkle corn-meal, stirring constantly, into rapidly boiling wate
Add salt. Stir frequently to prevent lumping. Cook 30 minutes over dire
heat. Serve with milk and sugar.

Leftover Cooked Cereals

Leftover cooked cereals, wheat, oatmeal, rice, cornmeal, barley, ma
be reheated, water added if necessary and used.

Cereals may also be put into a pan, cooled, sliced and fried in h
cooking fat until well browned. Serve with hot sausage or syrup.

Cracked or Whole Wheat Cereal

Sprinkle whole or cracked wheat into boiling water. Salt to taste. Boil for about five minutes and then set to the back of the stove so it cooks very slowly, about 4 to 6 hours.

Baked Beans

2 cups navy, red or lima beans
1/3 pound salt pork
2 teaspoons salt
1/4 cup molasses
1 cup boiling water
3/4 teaspoon mustard

Wash beans, cover with warm water, heat to boiling. Simmer until skins are easily pierced. Or take out on spoon, gently blow on bean, if skin splits and curls they are ready. Drain. Place scalded salt pork and beans in baking dish, combine molasses, salt, mustard and boiling water. Pour over beans. Add sufficient boiling water to cover. Bake in slow oven for 6 to 8 hours.

Beans may also be cooked in a dutch oven. Place the dutch oven in a pit with hot coals, cover with dirt and bake 6 to 8 hours.

Ham & Beans

Ham and beans can be prepared with any bean you might like. Clean and soak, overnight, the amount of beans you need. Drain. Add fresh water and cook until skins splits. When beans are ready add a ham bone, juice and pieces of ham. Season to taste and serve hot when done.

Chili

2 cups beans	2 tablespoons butter
1 medium onion, minced	1 1/2 pounds chopped beef
1 teaspoon chili powder	16 ounces tomatoes

Wash pinto beans and cover with 6 cups of water, bring to boil an boil 2 minutes, cover and let stand 1 hour, cook till tender. Drain. Me butter in skillet, add onions and brown lightly. Add beef, brown and coo at low heat for 10 minutes. Add beans, tomatoes and chili powder, sal and pepper. Simmer until thick and all flavors have blended. Serve hot.

Other dried legumes and grains -----

Split peas, lentils, rice, all kinds of lima, kidney, pinto beans, corr barley, wheat, garbanzo beans.

All of these can be added to soups, stews or cooked individuall and flavored to taste.

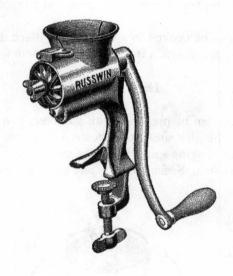

The End of a Perfect Day

Grandmother, on a winter's day
Milked the cows and fed them hay.
Slopped the hogs, saddled the mule,
And got the children off to school.
Did the washing, mopped the floors,
Washed some windows and did some chores.
Cooked a dish of home-dried fruit,
Pressed her husband's Sunday suit.
Swept the parlor, made the bed,
Baked a dozen loaves of bread.
Split some firewood and lugged it in,
Enough to fill a kitchen bin.
Cleaned the lamps and put in oil,
Stewed some apples she thought would spoil.
Churned the butter, baked a cake,
Then exclaims, "For mercy sake,
The calves have gotten out of the pen."
Went out and chased them in again.
Cooked a supper that was delicious,
And afterwards washed all the dishes.
Fed the cat and sprinkled the clothes,
Mended a basket full of hose.
Then opened the organ and began to play
"When You Come to the End of a Perfect Day."

GRIT Magazine, May 1990
Author unknown

The Outhouse

Aw, yes, last but not least. Now the outhouse was a very important fixture in the pioneer days. It beat running out behind a bush to do your "thing".

The man of the household generally dug a hole and built the outhouse. The outhouse was placed over the hole and was all ready for use. What happened when that hole was filled up?? Well, another one was dug, the house moved over to it and the first hole was covered up.

Now, the outhouse could be a one, two or three seater - maybe even more, depending how large t family was and how much company a person might desire to have whi visiting this outside convenience. Sometimes they even had two sto outhouses.

The outhouse was hot (and smelly) in summer and cold in the winte They could also be breezy if not properly built and placed. At night could be a cold, treacherous trip "out back" and was generally made at very quick pace.

The outhouse was one more thing that the housewife took care of. Sl saw to it that all of the chamber pots were dumped and cleaned each da and generally on wash day, after the washing was done, the wash wat was used to scrub out the little house to keep it clean and neat.

Now it is said that it is always best to place the outhouse downh from your house. After all, you are not in a hurry coming back! - *Myrr (Shafer) Carpita*

Cooking Terms

Blanch - to partially cook fruits or vegetables by placing in boiling water.

Dot - placing small pieces of butter over the top of fruit in a pie or casserole.

Dress - to remove internal organs of fish, poultry or game. To toss salads with salad dressing.

Fold - to mix carefully whipped cream or egg whites with other ingredients without beating.

Glaze - to coat exterior of food with thin mixture of spices, salt and/or sugar to add flavor such as a glazed ham.

Hull - to remove the green stem and leaves of strawberries.

Knead - mix and work dough by folding over, pressing and squeezing, usually with the hands as with bread dough.

Marinate - To tenderize and flavor meat by soaking in a mixture of spices, vinegars, wine, etc.

Pinch - Approximately 1/8 teaspoon of seasoning or spice.

Poach - to cook meat, fish, or eggs in a simmering liquid.

Puree - to mash solid foods into smooth mixture.

Searing - is exposing food to a very high temperature until the outer surface is cooked.

Score - To cut thin slashes on the surface of meats to tenderize or decorate.

Whip - to beat rapidly to add air and increase volume as in whipped cream.

Weights and Measures

2 1/2 Teaspoonful . . . . make One Tablespoonful

4   Tablespoonsful. .make One Wineglassful

2   Wineglassful . . . . .make One Gill

2   Gills. . . . . make One Coffee Cupful or 16 Tablespoonful

2   Teacupsful . . . . make One Pint

4   Teaspoonful Salt . . . . .make One Ounce

1 1/2 Tablespoonsful Granulated Sugar . . . . .make One Ounce

2   Tablespoonsful Flour. .make One Ounce

1   Pint Loaf Sugar . . . . weighs Ten Ounces

1   Pint Brown Sugar . . . . weighs Twelve Ounces

1   Pint Granulated Sugar. . . . . weighs Sixteen Ounces

1   Pint Wheat Flour . . . . weighs Nine Ounce

1   Pint Corn Meal. . . . . .weighs Eleven Ounces

1   Cup Uncooked Rice . . . . 4 Cups, Cooked

1   Pound Raisins, Seeded . . . . 3 Cups

10   Ordinary Sized Eggs . . . . weighs about Sixteen Ounce

A Piece of Butter, size of an egg . . . . weighs about 1 1/2 Ounces

To Remove Stains

Iron Rust - Hydrochloric acid. Lemon juice and salt. Sun.

Medicine - Alcohol. Soak.

Mildew - Lemon juice and sun, or make a paste of lemon juice, salt and starch.

Milk or Cream - Cold water. Soap

Mucus - Ammonia and water. Soap.

Paint - Benzene, turpentine, chloroform or naphtha.

Perspiration - Soap solution. Sunshine.

Wagon Grease - Lard, then warm water and soap.

Blood - Cold water. Corn starch mixed with water to consistency of cream, spread on spot, dry in sun, then scrape off. If not removed by first application, repeat.

Chocolate, Tea, Coffee - Borax and cold water, then boiling water poured through.

Fruit - Boiling water poured through.

Grass - Ammonia and water, soap and soda.

Ink - Milk and salt. Oxalic acid. Salt and lemon juice.

Tar - Saturate the spot and rub it well with turpentine.

Clean Iron Sinks - Rub them well with a cloth wet in kerosene oil.

Finger Marks - Sweet oil will remove finger marks from varnished furniture, and kerosene from oiled furniture.

The recipes used in this book are recipes provided by the members of the Jolly Jills Women's Club of Dillon, Montana or recipes from other resources that produced favorite foods they remembered but had recipes for. The beloved family dinners were prepared from scratch, with no written recipes, just a pinch of this, a handful of that. This is why we referred to old recipe books and collections to recreate the old favorites.

The lady of the household in pioneer days made due with very little, prepared hundreds of meals, knit miles of yarn, sewed yards and yards of material, gardened, milked the cow, took care of the chickens and other animals and many other chores in order to run her household and take care of her family.

Many thanks to the pioneer women and the individuals who have preserved the old recipes and told us of the many ways things were done and how they survived. We are so blessed to know the past and live in the present with so many conveniences that the early pioneer ladies could not even imagine.

Selected References

A Cook Book Containing Recipes of Quality - 1912
Maggie, by Myrna (Shafer) Carpita, copyright 1992
Montana Standard, Butte, Montana
Recipes From Many Lands, N.D. Homemaker's Club
 – date unknown
Tested Recipes, 1913 by the Ladies Aid Society,
 1st Baptist Church, Dillon, Montana
The People's Home Recipe Book by Mrs. Alice G. Kirk, 1913
The White House Cook Book, copyright 1887
White House Cookbook, year unknown

n addition, information was researched on the internet, from various
ʼncyclopedias, miscellaneous publications and oral interviews.

Index

CPSIA information can be obtained
at www.ICGtesting.com
Printed in the USA
FSHW011717040521
81092FS